CW00822682

OUT OF IRELAND

Mark O'Neill

Out of Ireland

By Mark O'Neill

ISBN-13: 978-988-8769-88-9

BIOGRAPHY / Autobiography

EB178

Published in Hong Kong by Earnshaw Books Ltd.

Contents

My Father, Desmond, drinking Guinness.

1

THE SECRET VOICE OF EAMON DE VALERA

THE MOMENT OF revelation came one December evening in 1962. My elder sister Patience and I were sitting with our Father, Desmond, round the dining table in our house in northwest London. It was in a basement room; the table was covered with yellow linoleum. My father had drunk two glasses of wine—calm and relaxed. Suddenly, he started to speak in a voice we had never heard before, a soft Irish accent.

"The ideal Ireland that we would have, the Ireland that we dreamed of, would be the home of a people who valued material wealth only as a basis for right living, of a people who, satisfied with frugal comfort, devoted their leisure to the things of the spirit ... That was Eamon De Valera (the Irish President), you know," he said. "Then, how about the Catholic Primate Cardinal John D'Alton? Listen to him. 'Ireland is the most devout Catholic country in the world, producing more priests than any other. Many of them go on the missions overseas."

Every phrase and cadence was perfect. Patience and I were hypnotised; we were listening to another person.

"Go on, let us hear other Irish personalities," we said. "How about the Ulster Premier?"

Suddenly, the doorbell rang. I opened the door; a neighbour needed milk. Just as quickly as he has slipped into the Irish voice, my father went back to the standard British accent he normally used. It was like switching the button on a radio. The Irish voice was only for us to hear, not the outside world. For them, he was a well-established British doctor, a psychiatrist with a long list of patients and the author of books in his specialty. I did not realise it at the time, but that evening was the start of a long journey in search of my Irish identity that is the subject of this book. Thirteen years later, it took me to live and work in Belfast, Father's hometown, and, a decade later, to Faku, a small town in Liaoning province in northeast China, where Grandfather lived for 45 years.

My father talked little about his early life. Born in Dungannon, Northern Ireland in September 1916, he spent his first six years in Faku, where his parents, Frederick and Annie, were missionaries of the Presbyterian Church of Ireland (PCI). Aged six, his mother brought him back to Northern Ireland for his education. They took the trans-Siberian railway and stopped off in Moscow; he recalled seeing sights of the Russian capital with his mother. He never went back to Manchuria.

He attended Royal Belfast Academical Institution, one of the city's best secondary schools, founded in 1814. He tried and failed to enter Oxford University, as his elder brother Denis had done. Instead, he graduated with a degree in medicine from Queen's University, Belfast. Denis went on from Oxford to a successful career as a civil servant in the Home Office in London. As far as we knew, while his parents were in Manchuria, Desmond lived in Belfast in the homes of friends or relatives. His parents came back for furlough, but the length of the journey and their reluctance to leave their congregation meant that these leaves were infrequent. In 1936, they came back for a full year; Grandfather was Moderator of the Church, a post he held for twelve months. At that time, they bought a one-storey home in Stockmans Lane, in the upmarket Malone district of south Belfast. My father lived with them there. In addition to his studies at Queen's, he studied midwifery in Dublin.

But he did not want to stay in Northern Ireland, and after his graduation, he went to London, to make his career in the centre of the British medical world. He had a good degree from a well-known university, but the medical profession was very conservative and his Irish accent a handicap. At that time, prejudice against Irish people was strong in Britain. We do not think he was able to find a medical job immediately after arriving in London. So my father did what many others had done before and since. He hired an elocution professor to learn the standard British accent that everyone heard on the radio. After three months' intensive work, he mastered it—and used it for the rest of his life. Thousands have done the same thing; they include both immigrants and those from areas of Britain with strong regional accents who wanted to make a career in the establishment. Edward Health and Margaret Thatcher, both Conservative Prime Ministers, were good examples. With this new accent, your origin could not be traced; it was the voice of middle class Britain. My father did not say why he decided to leave Northern Ireland. One explanation may be that he did not like its intense sectarianism nor the strict religious atmosphere in which he was brought up. He rarely saw his parents on the other side of the world. Both his elder brothers left Northern Ireland in their teens, one to go to Oxford University and the other to become an engineer in Sheffield, so he had little family at home. Another reason may be that he wanted to become a psychiatrist. In the 1930s, Ireland, both North and South, was a conservative country; its society did not regard psychiatry as mainstream medicine. It would be hard to work there as a psychiatrist.

On September 3, 1939, Britain and France declared war on Germany after its invasion of Poland. Within a few days, my father volunteered for the army. "Not only patriotism, but also a belief that the war would last a long time and everyone would be conscripted," he told us. "If you volunteered early, you had some say where you are posted."

In Northern Ireland, conscription was never introduced during World War II because of opposition from the Nationalist community. About 38,000 from Northern Ireland volunteered for the British armed forces; over 43,000 from southern Ireland joined up, even though their country was neutral in the conflict. My father joined the Royal Army Medical Corps and was assigned to 1 Battalion Irish Guards. The regiment had been established in 1900. During World War I, it won four Victoria Crosses; in the inter-war period, it served in Turkey, Gibraltar, Egypt and Palestine. During World War Two, my father served as a doctor in several campaigns including Norway, North Africa and Italy. The regiment lost 700 men killed, 1,500 wounded and was awarded 252 gallantry medals, including two Victoria Crosses. In December 1944, my father was awarded a Military Cross. After the end of the war, he worked for one year in Germany, treating traumatised German soldiers. Like many ex-soldiers, he rarely spoke about his war experiences, even when we asked him about it.

But we found in the British National Archives this citation for the medal from his commander, Lieutenant-Colonel C.A. Montagu-Douglas-Scott:

> "Captain O'Neill has been Medical Officer for this Battalion for over 4 years now. He has fought in NORWAY, TUNISIA and ITALY. In the first two campaigns, he was wounded during the course of his duties. During the recent fighting (in Italy), the Medical Officer has shown the most magnificent

> personal gallantry, and completely unselfish devotion to duty. He has been almost permanently under heavy fire and has performed all his various medical duties with a complete disregard for his own safety. He has gone out personally to get wounded men in on many occasions under the most dangerous conditions. He never wavered in his attention to the wounded despite the fact that the enemy were practically at the door of his Regimental Aid Post. During the whole of this time Captain O'NEILL showed the greatest skill and devotion and the Battalion owes him a deep debt of gratitude for the many lives he saved. I strongly recommend that he be awarded the M.C."
>
> What an impressive recommendation.

Family members told me that my father had chosen the most dangerous option. Since a doctor was a reserved occupation during the war, he could have chosen to work in a hospital in Britain; or he could have worked in an army hospital behind the fighting. Instead, he volunteered for a front-line battalion that put him close to the action and in the line of fire.

My father had an intense feeling of comradeship with those he had served with and of a time when bravery and dedication, not class and status, were the most important values in life. Every year he attended the regimental dinner. He also cherished the fact that the regiment included people from all over Ireland and was free of the sectarianism he had experienced in the North. Throughout his life, this remained his strongest link with Ireland.

After the war, he continued his medical career. He obtained a Diploma in Psychiatric Medicine (DPM) and became a member of the Royal College of Physicians. He became a physician in the Department of Psychiatry at a large National Health Service hospital in London. He also accepted private patients in his own surgery. He wrote specialist books and had articles published in The Lancet, one of the best-known medical journals in the world, the Spectator and other magazines. In 1955, Pitman Medical Publishing in London brought out his *A Psychosomatic Approach to Medicine*.

"This book is a brief outline of an approach to the patient that allows for the recognition of emotional state as well as physical condition", he wrote in the preface. It was about how stress disorder and other mental conditions affect physical illness. All this was a substantial achievement for someone who had arrived in London in 1938 with an empty pocket and nothing but a medical degree and an Ulster accent.

In September 1946, he married Mary Pearson, daughter of a well-known Manchester lawyer. The marriage was held at a Presbyterian church in the London borough of Poplar. Patience was born in 1949 and me the following year. Tragically, Mary died of breast cancer in 1955; treatments then were far less advanced than today. In the late 1950s, we moved into a spacious four-storey house in St Johns Wood, a desirable upper middle class district of northwest London; it had a garden at the back. It was in that house that I became aware of the life and society of which we were part. My father used the house as his surgery for private patients. So it was full of visitors—patients, secretaries, friends and the ladies whom he hired to look after me and my sister and manage the house. I scarcely recall meeting any Irish people. My father rarely met his two brothers and did not join any Irish club or social association. But he retained a close connection with his mother Annie, who lost her husband in October 1952; every week she wrote him a long letter and he replied, more briefly. He went to Belfast to visit her, on one occasion taking Patience and me with him. Once she came to visit us. I recall a small, talkative woman with a moustache. My father took her to a nice restaurant and ordered wine; a lifetime teetotaller, she was shocked. He spoke lovingly of her as someone who liked talking and drank a lot of tea; a minister and his wife met many people and tea was their drink of choice. After she passed away in November 1957, my father went to Belfast for her funeral. It was his last visit there. After that, his only regular encounter with Irish people was at the regimental dinner. Evidently, like many migrants, he had chosen to move on from his past and build a new life and career for himself. How successful he had been.

At one social event, in my early teens, I met a well-known writer called Brian Inglis; my father liked his books.

"Hello, Mr Inglis, you are an Irish author," I said.

"No, I am a West Brit," he replied.

I did not understand his reply. My father explained that, in 1962, Inglis had published a book "West Briton". Later I discovered that Irish people used this term, in a negative sense, to refer to those who stayed in Ireland after independence in 1922 but would have preferred the country to remain part of Britain. Inglis wrote a large number of books, many about Ireland. A native of Dublin, he had chosen, like my father, to leave the society in which he grew up and settle in London. There he became a successful journalist, author and television presenter; he was editor of The Spectator magazine from 1959 to 1962.

Another reminder of my father's past was a poster of James Joyce in his bedroom; with a flat cap, Joyce is standing with his hands in his pocket and, below him, the words "Silence, Exile, Cunning". I looked up the reference:

> "I will not serve that in which I no longer believe, whether it call itself my home, my fatherland or my church: and I will try to express myself in some mode

> of life and art as freely as I can and as wholly as I can, using for my defence the only arms I allow myself to use – silence, exile and cunning."

Is that what Father thought too? Like him, Joyce left Ireland aged 22, to a more dramatic exile – Trieste, Paris and Zurich. But Dublin remained the centre of his literary world; my father, on the other hand, turned his back on Northern Ireland. These – and the unforgettable De Valera speech – were the rare reminders of where my father came from. Otherwise, he lived the life of a successful British professional, respected by his peers and giving speeches at medical conferences.

From an early age, I developed a love of soccer. In our new home, I used to practice in the garden and gaze into the consulting room where my father saw patients. The sessions lasted hours.

"Is there so much to talk about?" I asked him.

"I listen and talk little," he replied.

In fact, many sessions went on so long that he had no time to see the next patient. Some ended up sleeping in one of the rooms of the house. At breakfast time, around the table with the yellow lino, I sometimes saw an unfamiliar face – that of a patient still waiting for their appointment. They were nice to me, as the son of their physician, and we chatted. One gave me a book he had written, thick and bound in hardback; when I opened it, I found that there was no punctuation or chapters. It was a small window into the complex and often fearful world of mental illness my father confronted every day. We had a father and son team who came to clean the windows. Soccer fans, they kindly took me to watch games at Fulham and West Ham – noisy and boisterous, another universe to the calm gentility of St John's Wood.

At school, I met no Irish people. I attended two expensive boarding schools, which my father had chosen as the entry ticket into the upper echelons of British society; the fees were expensive, putting them out of reach of ordinary people, British or Irish. We had a gruelling study schedule, including Latin and classical Greek, with sports and hours of classes and homework in the evenings; there was no free time. Irish history, society, literature and language did not feature in the curriculum. I had one classmate at the first school who had lost his father at an early age. His mother remarried a landowner from County Down in Northern Ireland and moved there. My friend recounted his holidays in its large house and estate. He had a younger brother, impulsive and adventurous. Later in life, I discovered that this brother had joined the Special Air Service (SAS) of the British Army and served in Northern Ireland at the same time I was there. Fortunately, I knew nothing of this. SAS members were on the front line in the Troubles: dressed in camouflage, they waited for days and nights in rain-soaked fields and hedges for their IRA prey. It was safer not to know what they were doing nor to have any contact with them.

So, in order to learn something of my family history, I had to go to the library and find books on Ireland – there were plenty. Thanks to them, I was able to gain a little understanding of the country's history and struggle for independence and the partition that led to the creation of Northern Ireland in 1922. One summer, a friend and I went on a cycling holiday for a week in County Mayo. It was a shock – while everyone spoke a language we understood, there was little resemblance to England. We cycled through areas of great beauty, with few people and derelict houses; motor vehicles were scarce and horse carts many. The dominant building in each village was a large church. We stayed in bed and breakfasts and had meals in the local pub. The welcome of the residents was warm, natural and overwhelming; we marvelled at their eloquence and gift of language. We did our shopping at small grocery shops, where there was little to buy. On the counter was a wooden collection box for the foreign missions, with a picture of an Irish priest surrounded by African or Asian children. It was polite to put something in, however little. It seemed a long way from the world in which I lived in England.

At university, I was able to read and learn more of Ireland's history. The Troubles in the North has just begun and gripped our attention. There were also parties to attend, sports to play, debates to listen to and exams to pass. I had decided to become a journalist, so I put much energy into writing for student magazines and arranging interviews.

In 1965, my father married again. Many of the family of my new step-mother lived in and near Edinburgh, so we spent holidays with them. Scotland opened a new page in my journey; I discovered the Irish footprint there was deep, and contested. A friend from secondary school was a native of Edinburgh and a supporter of Hibernian Football Club, one of the city's two big teams. Hibernia was the Latin name for Ireland. The other is Heart of Midlothian, after the novel of Sir Walter Scott. My friend took me to Hibernian games in the Easter Road stadium, in the Leith district. The atmosphere was lively and boisterous, but not violent. My friend hooked me on the team, a drug that has lasted until today. As the saying goes, "you can change your house, your job or your wife, but you cannot change your football team."

I looked into the club's history and found it very instructive. It was set up on August 6, 1875 by an Irish priest, Canon Edward Joseph Hannan. He was born in Ballingary, County Limerick in 1836 and ordained a priest in 1860. The next year he went to Edinburgh on holiday and was persuaded to stay by the city's bishop to run an Irish church and care for the many poor

Catholics there. The Great Famine of the 1840s had forced tens of thousands of Irish people to flee; many went to Glasgow and Edinburgh, the two largest cities of Scotland. In 1865, Father Hannan founded the local branch of the Catholic Young Men's Society (CYMS); many of its members played football—but anti-Irish prejudice was so strong that established clubs would not accept them as players. Father Hannan decided to give the members a club of their own. He was manager and president until his death in 1891. They chose Hibernian as the name of the club and green and white as the colours. But the Scottish and Edinburgh Football Associations banned their clubs from playing this new "Irish" team. Father Hannan lobbied hard and on Christmas Day 1875, Heart of Midlothian finally became the first team to play against them. Another followed three weeks later, and the Scottish Football Association grudgingly accepted them. Born into an Irish family in Edinburgh, James Connolly was a Hibernian fan; he became an Irish labour leader and one of the organisers of the Easter Rising in Dublin in 1916. After his capture, he was executed by the British Army. At the end of the 19th century, the club wisely changed the rule that players had to be members of the CYMS. It accepted players of any faith. Today the team still plays in green and white and celebrates its Irish roots. But is no longer seen as a Catholic or Irish institution; it draws fans from all over the community.

One Saturday, my friend and I took a 70-minute train journey to Glasgow to watch a game at Celtic Park, home of Celtic Football Club, in the east of the city. If Hibernian's Irish identity was discreet, that of Celtic hit you in the face. Their fans waved the Irish flag and their scarves were its three colours—green, white and orange. Their rich singing repertoire included the "Soldier's Song", the Irish national anthem. It was half a century after Ireland had won its independence; the intensity was as if it was yesterday.

It was Hibernian that inspired the establishment of Celtic in November 1887, twelve years after the Edinburgh club. The founder was also an Irish priest, Andrew Kerins (Aindreas O Ceirin), a Marist brother who took the religious name Brother Walfrid. He was born in 1840 in Ballymote, a village in the south of County Sligo. In the 1870s, he moved to Scotland, where he became a teacher and headmaster. Like Father Hannan, he wanted to help the poor Catholics of Glasgow; he founded the club to raise money for them. It played its first official game on May 28, 1888. In 1893, his order sent Brother Walfrid to London, where he organised football matches and charity for the poor Catholic children of Bow and Bethnal Green. On November 5, 2005, the club unveiled a bronze statue of him costing 30,000 pounds outside the stadium. The Archbishop of Glasgow blessed the statue and music specially composed for the event was played; the title was "Walfrid at the Gates of Paradise". This term was used because the stadium is close to the city's Eastern Necropolis; it is the occasion for many jokes – players who leave the club have departed from Paradise. The founding of Celtic was a disaster for Hibernian. In August 1888, one of the Celtic directors signed eight of its best players by offering them more money. The club went out of business; but it was able to re-establish itself. Like Hibernian, Celtic wisely accepted players whatever their religion, unlike their main city rivals, Rangers, which excluded Catholic players from the 1920s to 1989. It was hard to buy tickets for games between the two big Glasgow teams, known as the Old Firm; in any event, my friend and I were nervous about the level of violence, so we decided to stay away.

The nearest I came to Rangers was an interview in 1972 with Willie Waddell, one of their most famous players, when he was manager. On my own, as a student, I would never have been able to arrange such a meeting, but fortunately, I had a friend who was cunning and thick-skinned and organised it. Waddell was a short, thick-set intense man who had played more than 500 times for the team. The hot story of the day was whether Rangers would sign a Catholic, so we asked him about it. He did not answer the question directly but said that the club wanted strong, powerful and athletic Protestant men. Many of the club's fans supported the ban—probably the reason it did not lift the ban for another seventeen years. At that time, the most successful manager in Scotland was Jock Stein, the first Protestant manager of Celtic. He had played for Celtic for six years and become captain. As manager, he signed both Protestants and Catholics. In 1972, his team won the European Cup, the first time this had been achieved by a British side. All the players came from a thirty-mile radius of Celtic Park; it was a remarkable achievement. Scottish Catholics told me that this victory had an enormous psychological effect on them, giving them a self-confidence they had never felt before. Before taking up football, Stein had followed his father into the coal mines. His father was an ardent Rangers supporter who went to their stadium for every home game. We could not imagine conversations over the Stein dinner table at Sunday lunch.

The level of sectarian rivalry in Glasgow was like nothing I had seen in England. So it was time to turn to the history books again. Before the Great Famine, Irish migration to Scotland was seasonal, to work on the farms; after the harvest, the men went home. In 1841, just 4.8 per cent of the Scottish population of 2.62 million had been born in Ireland. The Great Famine changed everything. In 1851, the figure had reached 7.2 per cent or 207,000. They settled in places on the west coast, especially Glasgow, where almost 29 per cent of Irish migrants went to live. They worked in coal mines, docks and textiles, usually in low-paid jobs. They had their own schools, sports and recreation clubs; they largely married among themselves. Socially, they mixed little with the Scottish population. Since the Reformation, Scotland had been a strongly anti-Catholic country. The Church of Scotland was not Anglican, as in England, but Presbyterian, a sister to the PCI. In 1923, the Church and Nation Committee of the Church of Scotland issued a report on "The Menace of the Irish Race to our Scottish Nationality". It accused the Catholic population of subverting Presbyterian values and of drunkenness, crime and financial imprudence. It called for the ending of immigration of Irish Catholics to Scotland and the deportation of any convicted of a criminal offence or those living on state benefits. At the Old Firm games, the Rangers fans chanted: "The Famine is over, it is time to go home." This antagonism had intensified with the arrival of Protestant migrants from Northern Ireland from the late 1880s. In its 1923 report, the Church said: "No complaint can be made about the presence of an Orange population in Scotland. They are of the same race as ourselves and of the same Faith, and are readily assimilated to the Scottish race."

In Edinburgh, I walked around the campus of its famous university. I did not know it at the time, but the university contains New College, one of the largest and most famous centres for study of Theology and Religious Studies in Britain. It trains ministers of the Church of Scotland; many ministers of the PCI also studied there. The New College contains the General Assembly Hall of the church, where the annual assembly of the Church of Scotland is held. It is a strong and living link between the PCI and the Scottish church out of which it was born.

I was struggling to understand this religious conflict in Scotland, which mirrored the one in Ireland; I asked a retired Presbyterian minister to explain. "The Catholic church has too much power over its members," he said. "It bans divorce, contraception and abortion, which leads to large families. Most Catholic families are poor and cannot easily raise so many children. So they are condemned to poverty and emigration. Couples cannot divorce if their marriage breaks down; that is a mistake. In addition, the church is too exclusive. In a mixed marriage, it insists that the children be raised as Catholic; the church decides, but it should be the couple. It insists that the children attend Catholic schools. The history of Ireland has left a deep scar in Scotland. After 1922, most of the Protestants left the new state in the South. We feel a strong bond with the Protestants of Ireland, especially the Presbyterians. Their ancestors went there from Scotland."

In 1973, I moved to Manchester in 1973 for a job with Granada Television as a researcher for its current affairs programmes. By the Grace of God, I was introduced to a Scots-Irish couple, Joe and Ann McMurray, who rented me a room in their house. They were not only kind and welcoming hosts but also explained many mysteries of the Irish experience and helped me on my journey. Joe had graduated as an accountant in Scotland but could not get a job at a major accounting firm in Glasgow or Edinburgh, because he was a Catholic. "We were second-class citizens there and sectarianism is strong. So we moved to Manchester, where I found a good job and your religion is not an issue."

He and his wife were devout, attending Mass regularly; Ann worked for Catholic charities. He was also, it turned out, a fan of Hibernian and had an encyclopaedic knowledge of its history. Like Father, Joe and Ann were second-generation Irish; but, unlike him, they retained a strong affinity for Ireland and stayed in touch with their many relatives there. They had done well; they lived in a comfortable redbrick house and their three children went to university and became professionals. I was greatly touched by their warmth and openness.

In Manchester, I made friends with John Ware, a reporter with The Sun newspaper. He told me about his work – door-stepping celebrities and sleeping in his car outside their front door, as he waited for a telephone call from his ill-tempered editor demanding if he had secured the photograph and quotes he wanted. He gave invaluable insights into how the popular press worked and why it was so successful – not knowledge you can acquire in a library. In 1975, John was sent on temporary assignment to Belfast. The Troubles were in full swing. It was on the front pages of British and foreign newspapers every week. Once he arrived there, he called me: "You want to see a real news story, Mark? Come and spend a week with me here."

It was a great opportunity to visit the home town of Father and Grandfather; it was difficult to arrange without someone on the ground. I took a week's holiday from Granada and boarded a plane from Manchester. John picked me up at Belfast airport and drove me into the city. I was overwhelmed. On television, I had seen images of the city, but this was the real thing. This was not Bombay or Baghdad but a city in the United Kingdom. We saw bombed-out buildings, army foot patrols and the Royal Ulster Constabulary (RUC) in their jeeps. What struck me most was the "peace walls" – giant structures built to separate the housing districts of the two communities. The homes on either sides of the wall were the same – two-storey redbrick terrace houses of the working class I had seen all over the industrial towns of Lancashire. John drove along the Shankill and Falls Road, the main Protestant and Catholic working class areas. John explained the frontline reporting work he had done; I was full of admiration – by comparison, I felt as if I had been asleep during my journalistic career. We went for a drink to the Europa Hotel downtown; it was the most heavily bombed hotel in the world.

I had only seven days to grasp what was going on. Could I spend time in a Catholic area, to understand a little of the society and thinking there? John introduced a friend who kindly made a call to Father Des Wilson, a remarkable priest in Ballymurphy, a deprived Catholic estate in west Belfast that had suffered greatly in the Troubles. Father Wilson had moved there in 1966 and, unusually for a priest, lived in a terraced house in the district, not a comfortable parish house in a middle class area. He was very active in community development and education and worked as a mediator between different factions of the Irish Republican Army (IRA); it was a complex and dangerous role. By 1975, his relations with his bishop had broken down; he resigned. His pay cut off and forbidden to say Mass in a church, he continued to minister in Ballymurphy and said Mass in his house. Most graciously, he arranged for me to spend two nights in the home of one of his parishioners – a family of five – father, mother and three sons. I could think of no motive for his action other than to help someone. I slept in one room of their modest terraced house and stayed with the family during the day.

My education about Northern Ireland began. The father was a small, shy man who spoke little; he had been out of work for more than 20 years and had lost all self-confidence. His main interest was betting on the horses. The family relied on state benefits and the income of his wife who did cleaning work; she was the pillar of the family. She counted every penny. Their three sons were teenagers. "I am doing all I can to prevent them joining the IRA," she said. It was strong in the district; as I learnt later, IRA leader Gerry Adams was a resident of Ballymurphy. "Once they have joined, you cannot get them back," she said. "So I must persuade them there is an alternative path. So I enrolled them in the educational classes Father Wilson has organised and encouraged them to learn skills."

Even with skills, they, as working class Catholics, would find it hard to obtain regular employment, and the economy was in a poor state. The boys talked little; I dare not ask them about the IRA. I was moved by the warmth and hospitality of the family, who opened their home to a complete stranger. The three days were also an opportunity to talk to Father Wilson and the many people in his house. Everyone was friendly and informative, even to this person who had arrived out of nowhere. They showed me around the district, run down and full of people with nothing to do. It was a perfect recruiting ground for the IRA. The RUC did not go there; it was British soldiers, heavily armed, who patrolled.

It was an inspiring three days. The message was that, despite—or perhaps because of—being an outsider, this story was accessible. If I were there, I would be able to meet people and obtain information; that is the first condition of being a reporter. I asked John and his Irish friends: was it safe to live and work there? They explained that, after six years, the Troubles had evolved 'rules of engagement'. On the front line, most at risk, were members of the security forces, including army and RUC, those serving in the prisons and the justice system, activists and the paramilitaries on both sides. Also in danger were those who lived in areas of confrontation and could be caught in crossfire. Up to now, they said, journalists were not targeted; each side needed reporters to tell their story and regarded them as neutral. Be objective and do not get too close to either side, our friends said: be seen as neutral and you will be left alone. With this assurance, I thought that this was a rare opportunity, to report such an important story and learn for the first time about the land of my father and grandfather.

So I went back to Manchester and resumed work there. I watched for advertisements for jobs in Northern Ireland and found a vacancy in the BBC office in Belfast as researcher for Nationwide. This was a news programme that went out at 1800 every weekday, with a 25-minute segment going to the whole country and the next 25 minutes going to each region. The job was to inform the London office of the news each day from Northern Ireland and propose stories important enough to be included in the first 25-minute national segment. With only three years' experience in the profession and no detailed knowledge of Northern Ireland, I was not well-qualified. I applied and, fortunately, was given the post. I imagine that few people, perhaps no-one else, applied. For most people, Belfast in 1975 was not an attractive city to live. I thanked God, said my goodbyes to my colleagues at Granada TV and the McMurrays and prepared to leave. The next three and a half years proved to be a critical stage of my journey.

Belfast City Hall.

2

Learning

After I arrived in Belfast, I realised how little I knew. While Northern Ireland was, and is, part of the United Kingdom, it had a history and a present unique to itself. Like other people, I had followed the Troubles in the newspapers and on television, but when I got there, I saw how much there was to learn. Fortunately, I was blessed to meet many people to guide the blind man through the forest. They greatly helped me along the next part of the journey.

My new place of work was BBC Northern Ireland, a six-storey building on the corner of Ormeau Avenue and Bedford Street in the centre of Belfast. It had opened in May 1941; the building was in neo-Georgian style, steel-framed with reinforced concrete floors and sand-faced bricks. As it was the national broadcaster, its staff were accustomed to new people arriving to work in their midst with little background or knowledge of Northern Ireland. In the early months, my strongest feeling was a sense of inadequacy. With almost no local contacts, I had little news or information to offer my colleagues; my job was to listen and learn. I was given a chair and desk in the main newsroom. I was fortunate not to be on the front line. My job was to inform the London newsroom about what was happening in Northern Ireland and recommend topics and interviews for its national early evening programme. Each regional station—including the one in Northern Ireland—had its own segment. One early interviewee was a British army bomb disposal expert. "People, money and time are my priorities, in that order," he said. He gave a fascinating and moving description of how he dismantled bombs that had not exploded; one mistake could cost him his life. Another interviewee was the Northern Ireland "Nurse of the Year"; she worked in a hospital unit that specialised in plastic limbs. She said that, when she visited her sister in Dublin, she went dancing every night, but that, at home in Belfast, she had not been out for five years.

One person who helped me greatly was Roisin McAuley, a colleague at the BBC. Born in Belfast and growing up in Cookstown, County Tyrone, she attended a convent boarding school and graduated in history from Queen's University, Belfast, the same institution as Father and Grandfather. In 1969, she joined BBC Northern Ireland as its first Catholic female newsreader and announcer. During her time at Queen's, the students were in the vanguard of the civil rights movement; she was among them. This gave her a wide network of friends and acquaintances; some remained activists and went into politics and the media, others joined Sinn Fein and a small number joined the armed struggle. All this gave her an intimate understanding of what was going on, especially in the Catholic and Nationalist community. But, like most journalists, she had sources in both communities and in all political parties.

Roisin was extremely kind to the neophyte. She introduced me to many of her friends. Such introductions were invaluable in a society bitterly divided, which had made people suspicious of outsiders. She also provided help in two essential ways. One was where to live. She showed me a map of Belfast, painted red, green and yellow; I had never seen such a map before. Red meant a Protestant area, green meant a Catholic area and yellow a neutral one. Most of the killings occurred in the Red and Green areas, by paramilitaries from the opposite side or in confrontations between the security forces and the Nationalists.

"You are safer living in a yellow area, preferably close to Queens," she said. "That is the area where I live. It has been little targeted by any faction and is also close to the BBC and the city centre."

This was excellent advice; I found a room in a three-storey terraced house in University Avenue, walking distance from Queens, with four other young men. It was a street of modest red-brick terraced houses such as you could find in industrial cities all over north and central England. I lived there for the next three and a half years. I will speak more about my room-mates later in the story. I discovered later that my new home was round the corner from the house where Grandfather was born and grew up.

Then Roisin gave another piece of good advice – use a bicycle. Belfast was not a large city; most areas which we had to cover were within reach by bicycle. Its great advantage was flexibility. The police and army could seal a road or roads at short notice, often leading to long traffic jams; with a bicycle, you could turn quickly and find another route to your destination. It was also good when you needed to escape from street confrontations, between the two sides or between one of them and the security forces. On a bicycle, you could ride rapidly along the pavement or down an alley to a safer place. I used one all my time in Belfast. Going to work meant a pleasant cycle ride of 15 minutes, past Queen's University and the shops and restaurants surrounding it, and along the main roads leading to the city centre. Thanks again to Roisin.

With the new bicycle, I was able to explore. I started with the city centre. Most impressive was City Hall in Donegall Square;

it was built of Portland stone in the Baroque revival style. Fifty-three metres high, it opened on August 1, 1906. In front is a large statue of Queen Victoria. The building was a symbol of Belfast's golden age, when it was the largest and most industrial city in Ireland, with linen, rope-making, shipbuilding and engineering industries. It was an important manufacturing centre for the British Empire. Born in 1870, Grandfather grew up in what was then a flourishing city. Closer examination showed a sadder face. In the grounds of City Hall was the Titanic Memorial, a statue in the form of Death holding a laurel over the head of a drowned sailor. Inscribed on a plinth below were the names of the 22 Belfast men who died when the passenger liner, *Titanic*, on her maiden voyage from Southampton to New York collided with an iceberg and sank with the loss of some 1,500 lives. This great vessel, the largest ship in the world when it was launched from a Belfast shipyard in May 1911, has become, with the Troubles, what the city is most famous for in the world. In recent years, Belfast has turned this tragedy to its advantage, building a popular museum and hotel, as well as a new residential and commercial district, all named after the ship.

The *Titanic* was built by Harland and Wolff, then one of the world's largest shipyards. By the 1970s, when I arrived, the company was a shadow of its former self. But two of the company's yellow gantry cranes, named Samson and Goliath, still towered over the city skyline, 106 and 96 metres high respectively, a reminder of the firm's former glory.

Around City Hall, I found large commercial buildings, many dating from the Victorian era. They housed banks, law firms, accountants and other companies. There were streets full of pubs, restaurants, department stores and other shops. But the Troubles had disfigured this area. To enter a shop or building, you and your bag had to go through a search by security staff looking for weapons and explosives; you had to queue. This, and the regular soldier and police patrols of such a central area, did not make for a relaxed shopping experience.

Close to the city centre were streets that led to the epicentre of the Troubles – the Shankill and Falls Roads, the main Protestant and Catholic districts of the city. Both streets were full of black second-hand London taxis queuing up for passengers. These vehicles were children of the Troubles, I learnt. They had arrived in Belfast in 1972, after civil disturbances had driven many buses off the road. The city bus company had lost more than 300 buses, burnt out during these disturbances. By the time I arrived, there were 350 Catholic and 100 Protestant taxis, employing 900 drivers. They included sixty ex-internees and ex-prisoners who could not get a job anywhere else. The Falls Taxi Association (FTA), set up in 1974, owned two garages, an office and had eighteen full-time employees. The taxis carried up to eight passengers, for a flat fee less than the lowest bus fare. You could get on and off at the place of your choice. So the taxis were crowded with passengers, while the red and white city buses passing them were nearly empty. Each week the drivers contributed 2.5 pounds to the FTA, of which nearly half went to Green Cross, a welfare organisation for Republican prisoners. Over the next three and a half years, I took the taxis dozens of times. Everyone assumed that they paid a 'protection fee' to the paramilitary organisations that operated in the areas they went through. That way the drivers and their passengers would be secure. The taxis helped to enforce segregation. A Protestant would not dare to take one along the Falls Road, nor a Catholic along the Shankill Road. For a journalist, however, they had their plus points. You knew the 'tribe' of the passengers in the taxi and could ask them about the story of the day; you knew what not to say. Today, like the *Titanic*, the taxis have been turned to commercial benefit.

Tourists can hire one; the driver will take them on his original route and will describe with relish everything he sees along the way, making the visitors gasp.

After the city centre, it was time to visit the "Peace Walls" which had captured my attention during the first visit to the city, with John Ware, the journalist with The Sun newspaper. They were an astonishing sight in a European city, Berlin excepted. They were made of iron, brick or steel and were up to eight metres high. Some had gates, usually controlled by police, who allowed pedestrian or cycle traffic during the daytime but closed them at night. I found that they separated the Red and Green areas, especially the working class districts that were densely populated and close to each other. On either side, I found redbrick terraced houses, identical except for the 'tribe' of the residents. They told me that temporary peace walls had been built in the city in the 1920s and 1930s. These new ones had been constructed by the British army in 1969, to contain street violence between the two sides. Initially, they were temporary; but they were effective and so were made permanent.

Residents explained to me how this division of Red and Green came about. In August 1969, a Protestant mob burnt 270 houses, nearly all of them Catholic. This was the start of what became the largest migration of population in Western Europe in peacetime since World War II. Some 70,000 people were forced to move house, 80 per cent of them Catholic, to areas they felt safe. By 1974, this process of segregation was complete. One result of this mass migration was a worsening of housing conditions for many families. A survey in 1974 by the Northern Ireland public housing authority showed that nearly half the houses in the 17 central wards of Belfast, many of them Catholic, "were unfit for human habitation." Many had an outside toilet, no bathroom and were overcrowded, with Catholic families substantially larger than Protestant ones; families of eight children or more were commonplace.

The existence of the Peace Walls was another reason to use a bicycle, which could go through a gate, while a car could not. The walls were the front line in the conflict; two thirds of the deaths in the Troubles occurred within 500 metres of one of the walls. The residents told me that while most walls were in Belfast, other towns had them too – Lurgan, Portadown and Derry, as it is called by the Nationalists; Unionists call it Londonderry, after King James I gave it a royal charter in 1613 and its construction was funded by the London guilds. The walls in Belfast still exist today, more than twenty years after the Good Friday Agreement of 1998. As of the end of 2017, there were 59, stretching over 34 kilometres. The government wants to remove them – but a majority of those who live next to them prefer to keep them, for their own safety.

Roisin also helped me in a third way – an introduction to a choir in Andersonstown, a 'deep green' area of west Belfast. To grasp what was going on and the reasons for it, I needed to understand the thinking and experiences of those in the Republican community. Reading and interviews helped; even better would be regular contact with members of the community. So Roisin suggested this choir which held rehearsals two evenings a week and performed in churches and meeting halls at regular intervals. In this case, an introduction from a trusted person was essential. By now, six years into the Troubles, mutual hostility between the two sides had become intense and suspicion was strong. Most Protestants and Catholics did not dare to enter the areas of the other side, for fear of being identified there. They were willing to work in the shops and offices of the city centre, which was neutral and relatively safe. Factories were mainly in a Red or Green area; you worked in a factory in one of your own areas. Roisin's introduction enabled me to join the choir and attend its rehearsals and performances. Its members received me with great warmth and tolerance; no-one questioned my motives for joining. The visits achieved exactly what I hoped. I was able to make friends with the members and learn much about their lives, feelings and experiences, an important step toward understanding this complex situation. The regular performances, in front of an audience, were a treat. It became a twice-weekly routine. In the early evening, I set off on the bicycle through the quiet, tree-lined streets of south Belfast and along Stockmans Lane where Father had grown up. Then you crossed below the north-south motorway that marked the start of the city's main Green area. The atmosphere changed at once. Anti-British graffiti were painted on the walls and few people ventured out onto the streets. They were not as clean and tidy as those in wealthy south Belfast. You passed an army foot patrol or personnel carrier. Then I arrived at the hall where the rehearsals were held, to find tea and smiles – warmth to offset the cold outside. Cycling back after the rehearsal, I found the well-lit streets almost empty; time to be on the alert. Go quickly and do not linger. After I crossed below the motorway again, the tension fell and it was an easy ride home.

By now, I had begun to understand a little the rules of the game. Northern Ireland was – and is – divided into two 'tribes' – Protestant and Catholic. Most people lived within their own tribe. When two strangers met, one quickly learnt to which side the other belonged – from the name, where he or she lived, worked or went to school. In 1975, Belfast had a population of only 430,000; people knew each other well. Because of my British accent, I belonged to a third category – people from Great Britain. But I had an Irish name – one of the most common and one of the most famous. The O'Neills had been Irish chieftains;

I was of Irish origin, but my accent and behaviour showed that I belonged to neither 'tribe'. In Belfast, there were many such people from Great Britain—civil servants, teachers, those who had married local people and the military. The government did not send soldiers of Irish regiments to serve in Northern Ireland. For a journalist, this "third category" identity was good and bad. The upside was that I did not belong to one side or the other and could be seen as neutral and objective. The downside was that it was impossible to obtain access to the secrets, especially the military ones, of either side; neither would trust you enough. This was reserved for journalists who had grown up there. In any event, it was essential to be transparent and not hide anything—"having no trap door," as one paramilitary put it to me. In this atmosphere of bitterness and paranoia, anyone could be suspected of being an informer for a paramilitary group or the security forces—and become a target. We journalists also had the advantage that people could read or hear our work, often within hours; so they could see what we were doing. During the thirty years of the Troubles from 1969 to 1998, 3,532 people were killed, of whom sixty per cent were civilians. But only one journalist, Martin O'Hagan, was killed, in September 2001; earlier, he had served seven years in prison for firearms offences before becoming a journalist. So, according to the rules of the Troubles, journalists were not targeted. This was an enormous blessing and gave me confidence to visit dangerous areas.

After the initial months of listening and learning, I felt able to do interviews on my own. An early one was with Paddy Devlin, one of the founders of the Social Democratic and Labour Party in 1970; it was a moderate, mainly Catholic party; one founder member, Ivan Cooper, was a Protestant. In 1974, Devlin had served for five months as Northern Ireland Minister of Health and Social Services in a power-sharing government; it collapsed after opposition by the Protestant Ulster Unionist Party and a two-week strike and blockade by Protestant paramilitaries, who killed 39 civilians. It was the most important post Devlin would ever hold. A short, stout man, he lived in the Green area of Belfast for all his 74 years, except three years as a scaffolder and car worker in England from 1945 to 1948.

I cycled to his modest terraced home off the Falls Road. He showed me into his sitting room and sat on the sofa. It was not comfortable; I was sitting on top of a hard object. Devlin was nervous and asked me to move to another chair. He sat on the sofa and removed from below a cushion a gun—which I had been sitting on. A prominent politician interned for three years during World War II, he was a potential target for Protestant paramilitaries. That did not start the interview on a good footing. But he was an eloquent man. He spoke of his efforts to set up a strong labour movement in Northern Ireland which brought together working people from both 'tribes' in a common cause. Poor and disadvantaged, they were the greatest victims of the Troubles. In a normal country, such a movement would have been possible. But the special history of Northern Ireland had put the sectarian division above everything else. Like others, Devlin failed in his efforts to set up a labour movement that included both sides. In 1978, he set up the United Labour Party and stood as its candidate for the European Parliament in 1979. He received just 6,122 first preferences, 1.1 per cent of the votes cast, and lost his deposit. Devlin was a passionate and impressive man; he did his most productive work in the trade union movement.

One Saturday morning, I went to visit an American lady who lived in Ardoyne, a strongly Republican area of north Belfast. Its working class people lived in rows of red-brick terraced houses. It was always tense. British army snipers were stationed at the top of disused textile buildings that overlooked the streets. They were watching for any movement by members of the Provisional Irish Republican Army. Against this ominous background, mothers wheeled their children to the shops to buy milk and eggs and elderly people stood gossiping on street corners. The American lady, a lesbian, lived with her girlfriend in her house in Ardoyne. In this strongly Catholic neighbourhood, they had to be discreet about their relations. After an enjoyable coffee and conversation with the two, I got back on the bicycle and started to go home. Then a wall graffiti caught my eye – "Poland 1 England 1". This recalled a famous football game in October 1973; the draw prevented England from qualifying for the World Cup the next year – something for Belfast Republicans to celebrate. There were many such graffiti in the Green areas; they ranged from the comic to the malicious and satirical. One of the best-known was: "Is there Life before Death, Wilson?" Harold Wilson was British Prime Minister from March 1974 to April 1976. I liked to take photographs of these graffiti and stopped to take one of the Polish one. At that moment, a Morris Minor with four young men inside pulled up on the road. One of the four got out; he was wearing a baggy brown raincoat which could easily conceal a weapon.

"What are you doing here?" he said angrily.

"I was visiting a friend who lives in Ardoyne. I am a journalist."

"Where is your press card?"

I fumbled in my pocket but could not find it. "I am sorry. I changed my trousers this morning and forgot to bring it."

The man hesitated. He knew the army snipers were watching him from the buildings at the end of the road. He had two to three seconds to decide whether to throw me into the Morris Minor. "We will let you go this time. Now leave and never come back," he said and got back into the car.

It was a lucky escape. Once in their car, I would be entirely at their mercy.

That was Saturday morning. Ardoyne was a 'hot' area, a place of frequent confrontation. I did not want to be banned. So, on the Monday morning, I cycled back and walked along the street.

"Where is the Sinn Fein office?" I asked an elderly woman.

"There, it is number 34," she said.

Sinn Fein was a legal party and could therefore operate openly. I went in, showed my press card and explained what had happened. A man in his 30s took me into his room. He turned up the volume of BBC Radio One, a pop music channel, to interfere with the listening devices he assumed to be in the room.

"Very well," he said. "That is clear enough. We give you permission to come back to Ardoyne. But you must carry the press card with you at all times."

That was a very clear example of the privilege given to journalists during the Troubles.

> Here is part of a letter I wrote to a friend on June 22 1975, a few months after arrival. "It is hard to spot the centre of things … The rule of fear casts a giant shadow over everything public. The truth is spoken only in whispers, never published. This sense of different levels of knowledge, and ignorance, is continued. Three men shot in a car on the border, no apparent motive. This has a political meaning, a human meaning; also a military and a territorial significance, a move in a mysterious game. We do not know the rules but fear the consequences. The price of assassination is lower than a week's wages. I find the British, though not the Irish, journalists facetious.
>
> "The Newsletter, the main Protestant newspaper,

> does not carry the same stories as the Irish News, its Catholic competitor. Neither are the same as any of the numerous community papers. It is not the same country you are reading about. This is a sign of how this state of things could have lasted for 50 years. No-one was lying; they did not know.
>
> "You have never met people who converse so well, offering an infectious good humour and little kindnesses that make the English look like ice-boxes. Living is made easy ... This setting (close to Queen's University) is incongruous. It is a well-kept Victorian university with many modern additions and a fine reputation. Anywhere else, it would be. Placed here, it assumes other significances—the only neutral territory, a historical reminder of the city's finest years and the place where Celtic Studies begin in 1908."

Life in the house where I lived and the surrounding enclave was relatively normal. My four room-mates were from Northern Ireland; all had steady jobs. Two were Protestant and two Catholic; everyone got on well together and avoided talking about politics. The house dated from the Victorian period and had thin brick walls. In the cold winters, we huddled around the coal fire in the kitchen that was the centre of our social life. On the top floor, my room was the coldest; sleeping required thick pyjamas and several blankets. Since we were men, tidiness was not our strong suit; it was unwise to invite any of their mothers to visit. Of the five, the star was Billy, who lived in the front room; he was an accomplished Casanova. Often there were several ladies on the go at the same time; he left us detailed instructions of what to do if one lady knocked at the door while another was present. At all times he kept the curtains of his windows closed;

they faced the street.

"Sorry, Billy is out at the moment," I told one attractive lady visitor.

"But that is his car parked right here."

"Yes, but he had to go out urgently. Sorry, I do not know when he will return. I will tell him you called."

The lady was angry and suspicious; but she left finally.

Billy used to boast of his conquests, as many men do: true or false we did not know. I was not sure of his ethics; but, in one way, I found it reassuring that, in the middle of the killings and explosions, he could have this kind of 'normal' life. This was helped by the fact that, in our middle class Queens enclave, pubs and restaurants operated normally, with the addition of security men at the door watching who came in and out and what cars were driving along the street. The only difference with the rest of Europe was that, while customers told their jokes and stories, they had had to remain alert in case something happened. That is until later in the evening, when the beer and whiskey began to take effect: hard to remain vigilant in that condition. So we were largely able to have the normal social life of people in their twenties. Among the middle class, the two 'tribes' mixed more easily. But I observed that, for a partner, most people picked someone from the same 'tribe'; in that sectarian atmosphere, a 'mixed marriage' was too complicated and invited opposition from both families.

Some of the houses in University Avenue were rented to students and young people like us. Others were homes of middle class people; they were much tidier than ours. The front rooms were spotless, with a carpet, mantelpiece with family photos and sofa and two chairs covered with antimacassars neatly folded over the arms and backs. Curiously, while people lived in these houses, the front rooms were usually empty. One day I visited a neighbour, who kindly invited me for tea; we were sipping tea and eating soda bread in the kitchen at the back. I asked about her empty room.

"Do not be deceived," she said. "We rarely use it, only for the visits of the minister, other important people or rich relatives. That way it is easier to keep clean. It is the room everyone outside sees through the window. You want to give a good impression. The life of the family is here in the kitchen or the sitting room on the floor above, with the television."

How right she was—I observed the phenomenon of the spotless—and empty—front room in many houses.

Roisin went on to a distinguished career as a journalist and author. During the Falklands War in 1982, the BBC sent her to report from Argentina—an Irish citizen was welcome, but not a British one. Later she moved from Belfast to London, where she became a reporter for BBC programmes like Spotlight, Newsnight, Panorama and File on 4. She also produced and directed television documentaries for ITV and Channel 4 and presented programmes on BBC Radio 3 and 4. She successfully made the transition from Ulster broadcasting to mainstream British television; not every Irish journalist was able to do this. Unlike my father, she was able to use her Northern Ireland accent and did not need to learn an English one. Times had changed.

Roisin has also written four novels which have been published in the U.S., U.K, Germany and Holland. Then she moved back to Belfast, where she now lives with her husband, an English lawyer. She presents "Sunday Sequence" each week for BBC Radio Ulster.

All these encounters were invaluable to make, gradually, the picture of the birthplace of Father and Grandfather.

The Belfast school attended by my Father and Grandfather.

3

Looking for Father and Grandfather

After 12 months, I felt more settled and better informed in Belfast. I had a modest network of contacts and could contribute something to the collective knowledge of my colleagues in the BBC newsroom. So I asked to become a journalist with the local Radio Ulster station; my bosses agreed. It meant that I no longer reported to London but to the editors who produced news programmes for the local audience throughout the day. They gave reporting assignments and you proposed ones of your own. As a result, I was able to spend much of the day 'in the field' – carrying a tape recorder and microphone around the city, speaking to many people and visiting many places. This was an excellent opportunity to get to know the city better and broaden my knowledge.

In Belfast, I had another mission as well as work – to learn the history of my grandfather and my father which he had declined to tell his children. When we asked my father where he grew up, he said that he spent the first six years of his life in Faku, the small town in Liaoning, northeast China, where his parents were missionaries. In 1922, he returned to Belfast for his primary and secondary school education.

"My parents bought a small house on Stockmans Lane, which they used when they were on furlough (holiday)," he said. Such holidays were rare because of the long time needed to travel between China and Ireland, by sea and rail; in addition, my grandparents were reluctant to be absent for too long from their congregation. My father did not say so, but we felt that he was resentful at the long separations from his parents; why did they reserve their love for their Chinese parishioners and not for him? In a world without e-mail and long-distance telephones, his only contact with them was by letter, which took months to arrive. I later found that this sentiment was shared by other children of missionaries who served abroad. However much they respected the work their parents were doing, they could not forgive the silence and absences.

My father said that, when his parents bought the house, there were few houses on the street and they had no numbers. "So I named ours 23 and called it 'Innisfree', after the famous poem of William Butler Yeats," he said. The address was "Innisfree", Balmoral, Belfast.

In 1888, Yeats wrote "Innisfree", a 12-line poem, when he was living in London; homesick for his native County Sligo, he wrote about Innisfree, an uninhabited island in Lough Gill, where he spent summers as a child. During dark, miserable evenings in London, did my father feel the same way? The poem was widely praised in Britain and France, as well as Ireland. The name also eventually attracted the attention of the executives of Amore Pacific, the largest cosmetics and skin care company in South Korea. In 2000, they launched a brand of natural cosmetics called Innisfree (이니스프리 in Korean); it has become very successful, with stores all over Asia.

Stockmans Lane was easy to find; it was the route I took twice a week to the choir practice. It was opposite a large park. With the help of the residents, it was not too difficult to find the house – a small, single-storey residence.

"Your grandparents lived in it after they returned from

Manchuria in 1942," an elderly neighbour said. "After they died, none of their children were living in Belfast, so they donated it to the Presbyterian Church."

Born in 1916, my father came back to Belfast in 1922 and lived, we think, with friends or relatives. The church would probably have provided accommodation in mission houses when his parents were on furlough during World War One, but not for their children. From 1924 to 1926, my father attended the Killowen High School, then Malone Public Elementary School for two years and the Royal Belfast Academical Institution (Inst or RBAI) from September 1928. The family has preserved a copy of a report written by the principal of the Malone School on May 8, 1928:

> "Desmond Francis David O'Neill has been with me for a short time and has done exceedingly well. He had been in China with his parents for several years, and was, in consequence, badly in arrears in several subjects, but is now up to the usual standard. He has an excellent character and will give no trouble, his proficiency is good for his age, and if he follows in the footsteps of his grandfather, Reverend Dr. Wilson of Malone, and of his father, Rev. F.W.S. O'Neill of Manchuria, who were Instonians, he will not disgrace R.B.A.I."

When the family bought the house in Stockmans Lane, probably in the 1930s, my father moved into it. In 1936, my grandfather was Moderator of the General Assembly of the church, a position held for one year. He remained in Ireland during that year, before returning to Manchuria. After graduating from Queen's University in 1938, my father left the house and moved to

London. What was striking about the house was how modest it was. It belonged to a man who had been Moderator of the Church and served 45 years in a harsh posting overseas. Evidently, his reward was measured not in material terms but in the love of those who knew him, in Ireland and in China.

A short walk from the house was the imposing Malone Presbyterian Church, whose giant steeple still towers over the neighbourhood. It was the church my grandparents attended after their return from China in 1942. This was an important part of the family history, I learnt later. It was the church where my grandmother Annie grew up. She was the fifth of eleven children of Reverend Andrew Wilson, minister of the Malone church from 1883 to 1912. Growing up in such a religious family prepared her to embrace a missionary life in a poor and remote country; few young women would choose a husband in such a place. She went to China by sea in 1902 and married my grandfather in Shanghai, before they went to Faku. Malone was, and is, a wealthy area; the church flourished under Reverend Andrew Wilson. He raised 865 sterling to build a new church, which opened in June 1899; that is the one we see today.

I was still in the dark about many aspects of family history. Then I had a stroke of good fortune. The editor at the BBC sent me to interview Reverend Jack Weir, a minister of the Presbyterian Church and Clerk of the Presbyterian General Assembly, a position he held for twenty years. He was one of eight Protestant clerics who had held a secret meeting with the Army Council of the Provisional IRA at Smyth's Hotel in Feakle, County Clare in December 1974; they discussed a possible ceasefire. A small village in the west of Ireland, Feakle was chosen for its remoteness. The eight were brave men; no-one could predict what would happen, and the outcome could be violent. The IRA was an illegal organisation in both Northern Ireland and the Republic. Meeting its members made the eight ministers vulnerable to reprisals from Loyalist paramilitaries; one of the eight, Rev Ralph Baxter, later had to flee to Canada after death threats against him and his family by the Loyalist Ulster Defence Association (UDA). It was a desperate moment in Northern Ireland; its elected representatives had failed to break the political deadlock or end the violence. So Weir and his fellow ministers felt it was their duty to try. Unfortunately, someone leaked the news of the talks to the Irish government. The discussions had only just begun when heavily armed members of the Irish police stormed the hotel; they burst into an upstairs room to find the eight men with clerical collars. The talks did lead to a temporary IRA ceasefire for several weeks; but the Loyalist paramilitaries did not follow suit, and the war resumed.

Back in Belfast, Weir received many critical calls from members of his own community for "meeting the murderers". In my modest opinion, he was very courageous and did the correct thing. One of the other eight ministers was the Reverend Bill Arlow. Like Weir, he went on to work as a mediator for peace for many years. He said once: "It is better to fail in a cause which will finally succeed than to succeed in a cause that will finally fail." It is a good definition of faith.

My editor sent me to interview Reverend Weir about the Feakle talks. Against this tragic background, I cycled to the imposing headquarters of the Presbyterian Church in central Belfast. It is a Scottish baronial-style building built like a Scottish castle; it opened in 1905 and boasts a 40-metre-high clock tower modeled on that of St Giles Cathedral in Edinburgh. Since 1964, Rev Jack Weir had been Clerk of the General Assembly, making him the church's senior administrator; he would hold the post until 1985. He had a large office lined with wooden bookshelves. As he spoke of the Feakle talks, his voice was full of sadness. Like other ministers, he was on the front line of the Troubles; they met church members whose loved ones had been killed or injured. It was they who had to meet and comfort the bereaved – a most difficult and challenging job. A well-mannered man, Rev Weir asked me about myself. I said that my grandfather had been a missionary in Manchuria for 45 years. His face lit up, and the mood in the room improved dramatically. He said that he had been born in China and both he and his parents had also been missionaries there. His father died and was buried in China in a grave marked with a headstone which could not be found. Jack Weir left Shenyang only in August 1950, one of the last foreign missionaries to depart from northeast China. He talked movingly about his work there. Then he took me to the corridor with photographs of the previous Moderators of the Presbyterian Church. There was my grandfather, Moderator in 1936. It was the first time I had seen a photograph of him, serious and solemn. It was a moment of awakening, a connection with the past. That day I did not imagine I would have the opportunity to visit the home and church he built in Manchuria. Reverend Jack Weir himself would become Moderator in 1976.

After the BBC had broadcast the interview, I had time to research him. Rev Weir was born in Shenyang on March 23 1919 and received his primary education at a mission school in Yantai, Shandong province. In 1931, he returned to Belfast for secondary education at Campbell College and a degree in experimental physics before theological training; he was ordained a minister in October 1944. The following year, he went back to China and served as a missionary until his expulsion. He was just three years younger than my father; both had grown up in Manchuria and returned to Belfast for their education. Their childhoods were similar – separated from their parents for long periods and often on their own. While Weir followed his father's footsteps into the church, my father had chosen a different path; he left Northern Ireland and the church.

Weir went on to play an outstanding role in Ireland, promoting ecumenism and leading a Presbyterian delegation to meet Pope John Paul II during his visit to Ireland in September 1979. In 1992 and 1993, he and another Presbyterian minister, Reverend Godfrey Brown, held regular meetings with two senior leaders of Sinn Fein, the 'enemy'; each time the two men were taken to different houses in the Republican area of Belfast, each heavily fortified. For these meetings, the two were heavily criticised by Protestant politicians. Weir's response was: "It was a straight appeal for help, for them to help in bringing an end to the campaigns of violence which were bringing such sorrow and suffering, destruction and shame upon this province."

After I moved to Asia in 1978, I kept in touch with Weir and had the good fortune to meet him again twice. The first time was in Beijing in 1986, when he was en route to Manchuria. It was his first visit to China since his expulsion in 1950; remarkably, he had retained his ability to speak Chinese. He was greatly looking forward to seeing again those he and his father had served. I felt that he had prepared himself to spend his whole life as a missionary in Manchuria, like his father; he felt a strong attachment to the members of the church there. But the arrival of the Communist government had made it impossible for him to be there. We had dinner in a cavernous restaurant at the Fuxing hotel in Beijing; we were the only customers and were outnumbered by the staff. He spoke about the commitment of the Presbyterian missionaries in Manchuria and the fact that, except for serious illness, they could not return home. The terms of service were nine or ten years, later reduced to five, followed by furlough. A missionary came home only when he retired, unless he died early overseas, as had Jack Weir's father. It was a mission the church took very seriously. Homesickness, desire for family, friends and home comforts or difficulties in adapting to life and customs in China? These were not reasons to return home. If you did, you would be considered "returned empties", he said. The Weirs, like my grandparents, were tough people. Then I asked him about the length of the Communist 'dynasty'.

"Communism will not endure," he said. "It has no moral basis. It is amoral. Such a philosophy cannot survive."

Three years later the Berlin Wall collapsed and the countries of Eastern Europe abandoned Communism. How prophetic he was.

Our next, and final, meeting was in Towell House, a retirement home in East Belfast, where he had moved after contracting Parkinson's disease. It was spacious, with energetic staff, wide corridors and was full of greenery. Dr Weir showed us into his room. It was full of Chinese paintings and works of art. He showed us photographs and videos of his visits to China, including one in 1996, when his health was failing.

"I went against the advice of my doctors," he said. "But nothing could stop me going. It was a very emotional visit. I was born in China and lived as a child for twelve years. It is my second home."

Despite his physical discomfort, he was full of determination. On his bed was a cover in yellow and gold, with the shape of a dragon, a symbol reserved for the Chinese imperial household.

"This belonged to Pu Yi, the last Emperor of China," he said. From 1934 to 1945, Pu Yi had served as leader of Manchukuo, the puppet state set up by the Japanese in northeast China. "After the end of the war, everything belonging to Pu Yi became worthless. I found it at a flea market in Shenyang and bought it for a song."

His love for China and her people was very evident. He passed away on September 18, 2000, aged 81. How fitting it was that he should pass away below the bedcover of the Last Emperor.

That month, *The Guardian* newspaper published this obituary of him: "He dedicated his work and life to sundering communal divisions, promoting ecumenism and cooperation between the churches and, above all, opening minds and hearts to a much broader perspective than the narrow confines of Northern Ireland's highly dysfunctional and sectarian society ... It required courage, vision, leadership, dedication and faith, qualities Weir possessed."

My father and grandfather both attended the same secondary school—Royal Belfast Academical Institution, known as Inst. It was not hard to find. It sat, and sits, on an 18-acre site in the city centre, almost opposite the church headquarters where I had met Jack Weir. Founded in 1814, it was an independent grammar school that educated boys from 11 to 18 and had remained on the same site for two centuries. My father and grandfather were fortunate to be educated there. It was one of eight elite grammar schools in Northern Ireland and had a high academic standard, as well as sports, music, debating and other activities. Many alumni went on to important positions in the government, industry, medicine, law and the military. One was Thomas Andrews, head of the drafting department at Harland and Wolff; he helped to design the Oceanic II, the Olympic and the Titanic, the largest ships afloat. He was on board the *Titanic* on its maiden voyage and perished with so many of the crew and passengers.

My father spoke little about his studies at Inst. I later found correspondence between his teachers and his father, then in Manchuria, discussing his academic performance. Since a letter took three months to reach the other side, I wonder how useful these exchanges could have been. We found school reports from 1928, 1930 and 1934. In 1930, he was studying Latin, Greek, English, History, Geography, Mathematics, Physics and

Chemistry. A report by the school principal on October 24, 1933 said that he was in the Science Upper Sixth. "During the whole of his time here, his character and conduct have been excellent and his work has always reached a very high standard. I recommend him with confidence."

In any event, my father did well enough to be admitted to study medicine at Queens – but did not get into Oxford, as he hoped and as his elder brother Denis had done. He had a second elder brother, Terence.

At Inst, my father met a cross-section of society; entry was by merit and the fees were modest. But he had no Catholic classmates. This was another special feature of Northern Ireland. The Catholic church demanded that its members send their children to church schools. This segregation continues today – as of 2021, only seven per cent of students there attended integrated schools. Some Catholic parents choose elite non-Catholic schools for their children. Very few Protestants attend Catholic schools, which have a strong religious content.

During my time in Belfast, we always feared that Inst would be a target of a bomb attack. It was a well-known 'Protestant' institution in the middle of the city centre; it was a short walk from the Europa, famous as the most bombed hotel in the world – it was hit 36 times. The school had regular bomb alerts; all 1,000 students had to evacuate their classrooms and gather on the front lawn. But, remarkably, through the three decades of the Troubles, Inst did not lose one day of school.

Once we asked my father if he could remember the Chinese he spoke as a young boy in Faku. "Only two words," he said. "One is doufu (豆腐), soyabean, a staple food of people in Manchuria. The other is a swear word which I do not wish to repeat."

My grandfather, on the other hand, spoke Chinese fluently. He could give sermons in it. He debated with intellectuals who argued that missionaries like him had no business being in China and that its religions and culture long predated those of the West. Such debates required a command of academic words and concepts. Grandfather wrote three books about his life and work in Manchuria. I met a lady cousin who spent holidays in Northern Ireland after World War Two with our grandparents.

"When Grandfather became angry, he would speak in Mandarin," she said. "That way he could vent his anger but not upset anyone. No-one knew what he was saying."

Many missionaries do not return 'home'; they are buried in the countries to which

they devote their lives. The longer they stay, the more foreign they feel in their country of origin. My grandparents were forced to return home by the Japanese military; they put the two under house arrest in Faku after Pearl Harbour in December 1941. In July 1942, the two were interned and moved to Japan and put on a ship from Yokohama to Lourenço Marques in Mozambique, where they were exchanged for Japanese prisoners. From there they returned to Belfast, a long journey round the Cape of Good Hope. Without the war, I think, they would have stayed in Faku where their friends and congregation were. That is where they had made their life and their community; of their five sons, two died young and are buried in Faku. I wonder how comfortable they were back in Northern Ireland, where the concerns of people—outside missionary circles—were far removed from their life in Manchuria. My father told one story about Grandfather toward the end of his life. He went to his room after lunch, and should have been taking a nap, but when someone went to check on, the room was empty. The family rushed out and found him walking down the street with a suitcase, on his way back to Faku.

One day, in a newspaper, I read an article on the Irish nationality law which said that a person with a parent born on the island of Ireland was eligible for an Irish passport. So I obtained a copy of my father's birth certificate from the government office in Dublin, filled in the application form and sent it off. Several weeks later, a brown envelope arrived at our house. It contained the precious document, then dark green, valid from March 1, 1976. I have been using it proudly ever since, and have enjoyed the company of Irish diplomats around the world. That was a defining moment. Obtaining the passport of a country is no simple matter – look at the money many people will spend and the suffering they will endure to get one. I wondered what I had done to deserve an Irish passport; my contribution to the country was negligible. But there it was in my hand – the country had accepted me as one of its citizens.

A wall mural of Bobby Sands on a west Belfast street.

4

Violence

One Saturday morning, friends and I played football in a local park and had lunch in a Chinese restaurant in the Queen's University district. For a short time, we could have been in Bristol or Bordeaux. Then, on the radio news in the restaurant, we heard that the Provisional IRA (Provos) had bombed a furniture shop not far away; my editor called to say he wanted a story on it. We were back in Northern Ireland.

Sometimes the Provos sent a fax message to announce and explain a bombing, a killing or some other 'operation'. They were often signed "P. O'Neill"; we did not think he was an actual person, rather a collective name. Membership of the Provos was a criminal offence; if P. O'Neill was a real person, he could be arrested at any moment. But, on this occasion, there was no fax. So I cycled to a nearby Sinn Fein office to find out more. I showed my press card and was ushered into an office. A man in his thirties with short hair and open-neck shirt came forward; we assumed that, earlier in their lives, most of the men in this office had been "on active service" – taking part in IRA operations. They had served time in prison or not been caught. Now they had desk jobs in Sinn Fein; as a legal political organisation, it could have offices and spokesmen. The man was polite and gave me tea and biscuits.

"Why did you bomb this furniture shop (which included

three floors of merchandise)?" I asked. "What did the owner (a Protestant, we thought) do to deserve this?"

The man switched the radio to a pop music channel and turned up the volume, to interfere with the bugging devices he assumed to be in the building. "I cannot speak for the military wing," he said. This was the formula Sinn Fein people used; if he said he was a Provo spokesman, he could be arrested. "But let me explain. This is an economic, as well as a military, war against the British state. The IRA targets members of the British security forces, like soldiers and police. It also aims to make British rule of Northern Ireland prohibitively expensive, so that the Brits will withdraw. It gave advanced warning to the owner of the furniture shop, so that none of his family or staff was injured. The Brits will compensate him for the loss. The British government and public will ask how long they want to go on paying such compensation."

He was correct to say that after the bombing of shops and factories, the government compensated the owner, provided that he rebuilt his business to the same size as before. As best it could, it wanted to preserve the economy and encourage such businessmen to stay and not emigrate. We estimated that each year the Westminster government paid an annual subsidy of about three billion pounds to the Northern Ireland government, to cover the gap between its income and expenditure. That worked out at 2,000 pounds for each of the 1.5 million inhabitants a year. An insurance company would not pay compensation for damage caused by "riot and civil unrest." Such bombings traumatised the owner and his family. Economically, it was in his interest to re-start; psychologically, many did not wish to.

After the interview with Sinn Fein, I added information from the police about the bombing and the extent of the damage. I had enough material for a story. I did not attempt to interview the owner of the furniture shop; I thought he would be too traumatised to speak. During my time in Northern Ireland, I usually did not meet the victims and their families, although some journalists did. Instead, I interviewed those speaking for them, like priests, ministers, social workers, residents' groups or associations to which they belonged. These were the people on the front line; they met the victims and the relatives and had to confront their grief and their anger. They knew them personally, often for many years. We cannot imagine their pain and suffering. None of my family was killed or injured in the Troubles, nor anyone I worked with. I was very fortunate; I was shielded from the death and violence.

Once I went to stay the night with a distant cousin, who lived in the town of Dungannon, County Tyrone in the centre of Northern Ireland. I had never met him before; the evening was arranged by a mutual friend. When the O'Neills ruled a large part of Ulster up to the 17th century, they built a castle in the town, one of the highest points in the area. After Hugh O'Neill escaped to Spain in 1607, the town and castle were granted to Sir Arthur Chichester, one of the architects of the Ulster Plantation organised by the British government of that time. My father was born in the town, the family had relatives there. By the 1970s, it had a population of about 14,000, half Protestant and half Catholic. But the council was controlled by the Protestants; gerrymandering had put all the Catholics in one voting district, while the Protestants had two voting districts. Housing was unfairly allocated.

The beginning of the Civil Rights Movement in Northern Ireland can be traced back to discrimination in housing in Dungannon. In 1963, young Catholic mothers took a housing petition to the town council, in the first anti-discrimination demonstration in Northern Ireland. The Civil Rights Association

(CRA) rose from these beginnings. But the Unionist government at Stormont resisted the CRA's demand for fairness in voting and housing. In the first sectarian attacks in Northern Ireland, Protestants in Belfast attacked and burnt Catholic houses on Falls Road and Crumlin Road. The Unionist Government blocked all attempts at reform. The disbanding in 1970 of the Protestant Special Auxiliary Police force, the "B Specials" who had been implicated in attacks on Catholic areas, sparked rioting on the Protestant Shankill Road. This led to the death of the first policeman in The Troubles. Dormant and almost defunct, the IRA was revitalised. It attacked members of the British Army and the police force. Protestant Loyalist gangs retaliated by killing Catholics. Like many other towns, Dungannon suffered IRA bombing. People in and around the town were killed, a total of 33 between 1969 and 1993.

That evening I walked to the house of my cousin, down a pleasant lane with fields on either side. It was a one-storey property with a garden, green and quiet. He was a lawyer and worked in the family firm in the town. In normal times, he would have enjoyed a very pleasant life, but in Dungannon, things were far from normal. During our conversation, he revealed that he was a member of the Ulster Defence Regiment (UDR), was established in 1970 to replace the "B Specials" with the mission of "defence of life or property in Northern Ireland against armed attack or sabotage". By 1975, it had 9,000 part-time members, of whom my cousin was one. The vast majority were Protestant. They were a prime target for the IRA.

British soldiers sent from outside lived in heavily guarded barracks; when they went on patrol, they went in groups, armed and protecting one another. But the UDR soldiers lived among the general population and went to work like everyone else; people in their towns and communities knew who they were.

During the Troubles, 197 UDR men were killed on active service, and 61 killed after they left the regiment. Living in a single-storey house down a lane, my cousin was an obvious target. He took stringent security measures in and around his house; each morning he looked below his car to see if there was a bomb there. He slept with a weapon within easy reach. What I remember of that evening was his anger and bitterness. He was convinced of the rightness of what he was doing, and angry at how it had changed his life for the worse. What had he and his family done to risk death or injury every single day? The other thing I remember was his resentment against me, a relative; it was not stated but in the air. To summarise what was, I think, in his head: "How easy it is for you to come and stay here and return to your comfortable apartment in a safe area of Belfast. Your life is not at risk every day. In the evenings, you can go to the pub and a restaurant. At night, my men and I are patrolling the streets and country lanes, to protect people like you. What are you doing to help?" I learnt much from the visit, but did not think he wanted to see me again. It also made me think: If Father had stayed in Belfast, would he have had a life like this cousin? Would he or I have joined the UDR? That day made me happy that Father had decided to leave Northern Ireland.

For the security forces, one of the most dangerous places in Northern Ireland was South Armagh and especially the town of Crossmaglen, with 1,500 residents. Among its sons were Sir Thomas Jackson, the most famous chief manager of the Hongkong & Shanghai Bank, between 1876 and 1902; his statue stands in front of its landmark headquarters in Hong Kong. Another was Tomas O Fiaich, Catholic Primate of All Ireland from 1977 to 1990; the main square in the village is named after him. During the Troubles, at least 58 police officers and 124 soldiers were killed by the IRA in South Armagh, many in Crossmaglen itself. So this was a place to visit with extreme caution. The area was overwhelmingly Catholic. The Irish Boundary Commission of 1925 recommended that it be included inside the Republic of Ireland, to which it was adjacent; that is what the large majority of its residents wished. But the three governments involved—Dublin, London and Belfast—did not follow the recommendations of the commission; the whole county of Armagh remained in Northern Ireland, including Crossmaglen. The aim of the Unionists in Northern Ireland and at Westminster was to establish the largest land area which could support a Protestant majority. So six of the nine counties of Ulster became Northern Ireland. In South Armagh, the IRA was strong and active, with the support, voluntary or otherwise, of most of the population. In response, the British Army established a base in the town.

Because of all that was going on there, journalists had to report on the town; I was one of them. The best I could do for a contact was a reporter with a local newspaper who agreed to meet me in a pub.

"The situation here is very tense," he said. "When soldiers go into the town shops, the staff refuse to serve them, out of hatred or fear or both. The army base occupies the pitch of the Crossmaglen Rangers, the successful local Gaelic football team. That makes for even more resentment. It is too dangerous to supply the army base here by road, so everything has to be brought in by helicopter."

I walked around the small town; it had one- and two-storey buildings and narrow streets. There were few people and few vehicles outside. I imagined that armed men, in uniform and out of it, were watching the streets. An army patrol appeared; armed, the eight members walked briskly, looking in front, at back and to the side. Driving on the road next to them was a truck, allowing for a quick escape if needed.

The terrain of South Armagh was unfavourable to the army – rolling hills, country lanes, woods and farmland, ideal for the IRA to set up ambushes. The army used observation posts close to the nearby border to prevent attacks from the south. Since the posts were only manned some of the time, they were vulnerable. On August 13, 1974, two soldiers were killed when the IRA set off a bomb by remote control on their hilltop observation post three kilometres from Crossmaglen.

My visit there was an attempt to learn more about the abduction and murder of a captain in the Grenadier Guards named Robert Nairac, who was carrying out intelligence work in South Armagh. Among his fellow soldiers, he was unusual. A Catholic educated at Ampleforth College and Lincoln College Oxford, he was a successful boxer for the university. In July 1973, after graduating from the Royal Military Academy in Sandhurst, he was sent to Belfast. He was based in Ardoyne, a strongly Republican area. At the end of his posting, his battalion was sent to Hong Kong, but rather than go there, he volunteered for military intelligence duties in Northern Ireland and served a further 18 months. He went undercover – the most dangerous mission a British soldier could undertake; he was on his own in a place controlled by those whose objective was to kill people like him. It was both heroic and foolhardy. He mastered a Belfast accent, with the terms and slang used by people in Nationalist areas – the opposite of my father who hid his Irish identity, while Nairac concealed his British one. After finishing his tour in mid-1975, Nairac was promoted to the rank of Captain. Then he volunteered for a fourth tour of Northern Ireland.

On the evening of May 14 1977, Nairac drove alone to "The Three Steps", a pub in Dromintee, a village close to the border in South Armagh; he drove a civilian car and was wearing a donkey jacket and jeans. He pretended to be a member of the Official IRA from Ardoyne in Belfast. He sang "The Broad Black Brimmer of the IRA", accompanied by the band in the pub. He was putting his head into the mouth of the tiger. As a stranger, he aroused suspicion; it was a warm night, and he did not remove his heavy jacket. He was suspected of being a Protestant loyalist from Belfast, possibly reconnoitering the pub. An IRA man in the crowded pub became suspicious and asked others to help apprehend him. Three, including the IRA man, tackled him in the car park. The men had been drinking, but Nairac was sober. Then his gun fell out of his coat, blowing his cover. The men panicked and drove him the short distance across the border to Ravensdale Forest. They were joined by three other IRA members, one armed with a gun. It was a black farce of an interrogation, with the men stumbling around drunkenly in the dark. They were convinced Nairac was a UDA spy from the Shankill; he maintained until the end that he was a Catholic from Ardoyne. He was violently interrogated, punched and pistol-whipped. At one point, he wrested his own gun back from them and shot one of his attackers in the foot. They beat him over the head with a fence post. One abductor posed as a priest to try to get information. Nairac's last words to him: "Bless me, Father, for I have sinned." His captors lost patience and shot him dead; he was just 28. The men dispersed; the three IRA men stayed to dispose of the body, then escaped.

It was only when the abductors heard a BBC news bulletin the following morning that they realised they had shot a British soldier. His car was found in the car park of the pub in Dromintee. The army appeared to have no idea where he had been going, or why.

Journalists were trying, with difficulty, to understand many strange aspects to the killing. How was so valuable a soldier as

Nairac allowed to operate on his own in one of the most dangerous places in Northern Ireland? Did his superiors know where he was? Was he operating on his own? Were there not better ways of collecting intelligence? My meetings in Crossmaglen threw little light on these questions. Those who had the answers were few, and high up in British intelligence and the IRA – far above my pay grade. But at least the visit provided "colour", as journalists say; I could describe the geography of the South Armagh and the extreme tension which gripped the area, even if I had little to add to the main story. I was happy to return to the comparative safety of Belfast.

In November that year, a 24-year-old IRA member from the area confessed to the Irish police that he had killed Nairac.

"I shot the British captain," he said. "He never told us anything. He was a great soldier."

In 1978, the Royal Ulster Constabulary arrested five more men from South Armagh in connection with the case; they served prison terms. In February 1979, Nairac was posthumously awarded the George Cross.

Belfast Journalist Roisin McAuley gives this description of Nairac after she went to England to talk to his family, teachers and friends:

> *"I got the impression of a romantic, a dreamer, a T.E. Lawrence or Roland Leighton figure. He liked acting. He was a great mimic. He had kept a falcon at school. He had a romantic view of history. He wrote essays that were more fantasy than fact, featuring knights in armour and daring deeds. The shelves in his bedroom were lined with boys' adventure stories and books by Bulldog Drummond and Edgar Wallace about English gentlemen defeating foreign thieves.*

> *"He had boxed at Ampleforth, had wanted to give it up, but instead went on to become not just a boxing blue at Oxford but a boxer who would go on fighting even when he had taken too much punishment and the bout should have been stopped.*
>
> *"His grieving parents had little idea of Ireland or its history. South Armagh might as well have been beyond the Chindwin. In their view, he had been abroad, doing his duty. They spoke of his love of the English countryside, of wild things. His mother asked me to tell her about the place where he died. I described the field, the woods nearby, spring flowers, a small, stone bridge over a stream. She showed me a photograph of her son in his Grenadier Guards uniform, talking to a group of boys in Ardoyne. 'He could tame anything,' she said. Perhaps he thought he could tame Ireland.*
>
> *"At a 60th birthday party some years ago, I found myself sitting beside a former soldier in the Grenadier Guards. He had known Robert Nairac. 'He was allowed too much leeway,' he said. 'We all liked him.' Neither statement surprised me."*

It was an autumn afternoon in County Fermanagh, a county in the southwest of Northern Ireland. I was driving my Mini car back from a weekend with a friend in County Roscommon, over the border in the Republic. Uneasy to drive in the dark through such areas, I left my friend's house about 2 p.m.; to Belfast, it was a journey of two and a half hours. It was a country area, with rolling fields, scattered farmhouses and few people. I saw two young men ahead on the side of the road hitching a lift. Happy to have company, I stopped the car and let them in. They wanted to go to Belfast; they had thick Belfast accents. After a few minutes,

I opened the conversation.

"Where do you work?"

"We have not been working for several years," one said. This was not unusual in the poorer districts of Belfast. "How did you pass the time?"

After a pause, one said: "We were in Long Kesh."

Also known as the Maze, this was a maximum security prison 14 kilometres southwest of Belfast, where the government kept paramilitary prisoners from both sides.

"How was life in Long Kesh?" I asked.

The two were members of the IRA who had been "special category prisoners". This was a status given by the British government in July 1972 after a hunger strike by forty IRA prisoners. It meant that they were treated as prisoners of war; they did not have to wear prison uniform or do prison work.

"The screws (prison officers) did not have the right to enter our area," one said. "They left the food in trays at the door and we collected it." Life inside the prison dormitories was regulated by the IRA commanders. "Our time was highly organised. We had classes, including Gaelic, international politics and handcraft. We had sports and physical education."

Suddenly, one of the men looked ahead at the hill toward which we were heading.

"Green Howards," he said, referring to a regiment of the British army.

I strained my eyes and could just make out four men in uniform manning a checkpoint at the top of the hill. I wondered how the two men knew to which regiment the four belonged. They became very tense.

"What do we do now?" I asked.

"Pull up twenty feet ahead of the checkpoint, get out of the car and walk toward them," one said "Be friendly and make conversation. That will disarm them. A person sitting is in authority, while the person standing or leaning over is the suppliant. By getting out, you put them in authority. Do not let them talk to us."

That is what I did. I stopped the car twenty feet ahead of the soldiers, got out and went to talk to them in a friendly way. I asked them how busy they were and how they were enjoying the warm autumn weather. Their mission was to check cars for guns, explosives and wanted people; they did not expect this simpleton with a British accent to make silly conversation. They smiled and chatted for a few minutes.

"You can get back into the car now and drive on," they said.

The distance of twenty feet prevented the soldiers from having a good look at the two; they were tense and nervous, as the soldiers would have noticed. So we drove on, without difficulty. For the rest of the journey, the two men gave more details of the life of 'special category' prisoners in Long Kesh; I had enough material for a detailed story on a subject that was at that time not well known to the public. From what I could discern, the two men had served their time "for the cause" and wanted to return to a normal life. But that was not so simple. Joining the IRA was like joining the Mafia, a drug cartel or any other criminal organisation. With their cv, they would not find work in any government department or Protestant company. They would have to stay inside the Nationalist community; even within it, many would reject them because of what they had done. With such a record, legal emigration to another country was impossible. As the dusk fell, we were approaching Belfast. I trembled a little; if they had a weapon and demanded the car, I would give it to them. But they only asked to be let off close to Andersonstown, which I did. "Thank you for the ride," they said with a smile. I thanked God for the company and the safe arrival.

In March 1976, the British government announced the end of Special Category Status for those convicted of terrorist offences. Those who already had it would retain it, but no new prisoners would be granted the status from March 1. This set the stage for one of the biggest news stories during the second half of my time in Northern Ireland. In September that year, a new prisoner began what came to be called the "blanket protest". He and other Republican prisoners refused to wear prison uniform and went naked or made clothes out of prison blankets. We journalists found it hard to make sense of what was going on. Was prison not punishment enough? By May 1978, there were 301 Republican prisoners "on the blanket"; they had been sentenced for crimes committed after March 1976. The bed frames, tables and chairs had been removed from the cells; they were locked in 24 hours a day, without television, radio, newspapers or books except for the Bible and "Lives of the Saints." Here is part of a report I wrote for *The Observer* newspaper of London on May 5, 1978:

> "Corridors of two wings of H-block in the Maze are covered in urine and excreta. Several times a day prison officers in rubber boots and rubber gloves have to hose the corridors down with disinfectant and prison orderlies with gas masks mop up the mess. Their efforts are to no avail, since the prisoners have been pouring their slops through the smashed cell-door peepholes and windows. At the end of last week, when the peepholes were repaired, the prisoners poured urine under the door."

We could not enter the Maze nor interview the prisoners. The best we could do was to meet priests allowed to see them. The visits were stressful for them—listening to the anger and pain of the prisoners and trying to help them maintain a minimum of spiritual health. Being the priest of IRA prisoners also carried the risk of becoming a target of Loyalist paramilitaries. Those priests were sympathetic to the cause of the prisoners. The best known was Father Denis Faul, a teacher of Latin and religion at St Patrick's Boys Academy in Dungannon. As early as 1968, he became active in the civil rights movement. He protested abuses by the British army and the RUC; he also condemned killings by the IRA. He became the voice of the prisoners. What we learnt from Father Faul and spokesmen of Sinn Fein was the thinking of the prisoners: they were soldiers in a war with the British government and deserved to be treated as prisoners of war, as they were between 1972 and 1976. They wanted a return to the status quo of that period – no prison work or uniform and the right of free association with other prisoners and to organise educational classes and recreation.

One priest described to me the miserable conditions in the prison and said: "They have no means left. They are fighting British rule with their excrement." As the protests spread in the wider community, the IRA shot and killed prison officers. Protestant paramilitaries killed activists who supported the prisoners. Murals praising them appeared on the red-brick walls of streets in Catholic areas of Belfast. In Protestant areas, counter murals appeared: "The murderers have a choice. Their victims had none." And "Die in your 'H'ungry block".

When we asked Unionists for their opinion, their response was very clear. "We strongly support what the government is doing," one said. "These men have been found guilty of terrorist offences like murder, planting bombs and damaging people and property. They are criminals and must be treated like other prisoners." They found repulsive the images of men with long beards wrapped in a blanket in a room soiled with excrement.

Like other journalists, I felt sad and helpless as I watched this latest tragedy in the Northern Ireland story that brought death and suffering to everyone involved and to their families.

It was in 1981, after I had left Belfast, that the next, and most famous, episode of this story took place. On March 1, Bobby Sands, an IRA prisoner in the Maze, began a hunger strike. Initially, this did not attract wide support from the Republican community. Then, on April 9, Sands won a by-election for Sinn Fein in the Fermanagh and South Tyrone seat for the British Parliament, with 30,492 votes, despite never having campaigned there. As a prisoner, he could not go to Westminster; and, even if he were out of prison, it was the policy of Sinn Fein not to take seats in the British Parliament. On May 6, he died in the prison hospital on the 66th day of his hunger strike, and more than 100,000 people lined the route of his funeral. In July that year, the families of some of the strikers asked Father Faul to intervene. He was able to persuade the mothers of the prisoners to intervene and allow medical intervention when the prisoners fell into a coma. The strike ended on October 3. In total, ten Republican prisoners, all in their twenties, starved themselves to death, without obtaining concessions from the government. The campaign was a failure; apart from the votes for and the funeral of Bobby Sands, it did not arouse wide support in the Republican community in Ireland or abroad. I learnt later that the IRA leadership was against the hunger strike and that it was led from the outset by the prisoners themselves.

The lot of the 1,600 prison officers was scarcely better, as I found out when I met several of them. They told me the only attraction of the job was money—over 8,000 pounds a year, including allowances and as much overtime as they wanted. Those who came from England earned a 50-pound-a-month "bounty" and travel allowance; one worked four years in the N.I.

prisons and earned enough to buy a hotel in England for 16,000 pounds. One complained bitterly about the special category prisoners. "They can do what they like in the compounds. I sometimes wonder who runs the prison, they or the governor," one said. Another said: "There is no job satisfaction; all we can do is contain the prisoners. We cannot get to know them, we cannot help them. It is a very boring job. When I got home at night as a fireman, I used to feel that I had achieved something. I do not now." As of December 1977, six prison officers had been murdered by the Provisionals. "We are as much prisoners as they are," said a third. "They know where I live. I do not know how they find out, perhaps other prison officers, perhaps someone in the Northern Ireland Office. If we are holding a staff meeting, the prisoners can tell you exactly what is going to be talked about. It's uncanny." A Catholic, especially one who lived in a Republican area, would scarcely dare to join the Prison Service; so it was predominantly Protestant. During 1975, one in five of the officers left the service; in 1976, it was one in three.

During my time, the authorities made a small concession to the prisoners. They allowed conjugal visits, during which prisoners could meet their wives in privacy for a limited period. This resulted in a number of babies being born. I asked the British Sunday paper "News of the World" if they would like a story on these "babies behind the wire". The editor said: "Fine, but we must have a picture of the mother and the baby." Sinn Fein was happy to arrange such an interview.

One Saturday morning I drove with a photographer to a drab public housing estate in west Belfast and the home of the prisoner. He was serving a ten-year sentence in the Maze for arms offences. At the door was his wife, in her early 20s, her mother—and baby Sean, 10 months old. We sat down in the living room; on the walls were leather bags and purses made by IRA prisoners and sold as "Troubles" souvenirs. They kindly served tea and cakes. His wife was very talkative and proud of the little Sean.

"His father may be behind bars, but Sean will continue his struggle in the future," she said. "He will be a brave Republican soldier, like his father."

She described the childhood of herself and her husband – a large family in a working class district of west Belfast: poverty, limited education and work opportunities: alienation from the government and the police: strong Republican beliefs. This made her husband an easy recruit for the IRA in his teens; he was soon sent into "active service". His was a common story. Paramilitaries on both sides used the alienation and lack of opportunities of young men to recruit them. As she was talking, I had the picture for the newspaper in my head – she holding Sean, with the IRA purses on the wall behind her. After an hour's conversation, I asked if we could take a picture. She agreed and I went outside to bring in the photographer; out of caution, I had left him in the car during the interview. We came into the house and he was setting up the shot. Mother sat in a chair with Sean on her knee. All was ready. Suddenly, her mother spoke.

"No, do not agree to this," she said angrily. "They are laughing at us."

"Not at all," I said. "We want to show how the struggle continues even with your husband in prison."

But Mother was insistent and would not allow the picture. We thanked them for their time and left. Back home, I called the editor at the News of the World and said we had a good interview.

"Fine," he said. "How about the picture?"

"No, they did not agree to that."

"Sorry, mate, no picture, no story. Better luck next time."

An IRA poster on a Belfast street.

5

Rackets & Black Humour

It was mid-morning and I was cycling along a street in south Belfast. Suddenly I heard a large explosion and saw a cloud of smoke arising from a nearby road. I cycled toward it. It looked as if a retail shop had been targeted. Walking in the road in front of me was a well-dressed man with a suit and a briefcase.

"Do you know what happened here?" I asked him.

"Not yet, but I will find out soon. I am a loss assessor. I need to find the owner as soon as possible. In our office, we keep the radio on all the time to learn the latest incidents. We must reach the scene before our competitors."

This was the first time I had met such a person. His job was to persuade the victim of a bomb attack to hire his firm to make the application for compensation from the British government. The government paid such money in order to keep the Northern Ireland economy afloat and persuade business people to keep operating. Insurance companies in Ireland, as elsewhere, excluded "riot and civil unrest" from their policies. Both the government and the business owner appointed assessors to work out the damage. This was straightforward for large companies that kept detailed records of stocks and trading; but it was not so easy for family firms without the necessary staff, money and software. The largest single payment was 5.5 million pounds to Belfast's main department store, the Co-operative Society, after an enormous bomb and fire in 1972. Three days before it was due to open, another bomb went off. But damage was slight and the re-opening was delayed for only three weeks. The average waiting time for a claim to be settled was 68 weeks. Up to May 1978, the British government had paid out more than 500 million pounds for property and personal compensation—330 pounds for every man, woman and child in Northern Ireland.

The compensation applied for depended on the extent of the losses. By the time I reached Belfast, loss assessing had become a competitive business. That was why the man I met was in such a hurry to reach the scene; he had to make contact with the owner and persuade him or her to sign the contract with him first, before rival firms arrived. That was perfectly legitimate—the owner wanted to rebuild his business and the government wanted to keep the bruised economy going. But not everyone was honest—the newspapers reported fraud cases. The courts sentenced owners and assessors to prison for over-reporting the stocks that had been destroyed; they used fake and inaccurate receipts. To increase the claim of his client, one assessor invented a company with bogus trading records. There were even cases in which the owners themselves paid for a bombing in order to get compensation. In one case, a pharmacy presented receipts from a vendor in Scotland that were numbered one after another but dated six months apart. In other words, the vendor had no other client in that six-month period—an easy fraud to spot. The inspectors caught that one, but how many did they not catch?

This opened a window into one reason why the Troubles lasted three decades—rackets and money-making. The IRA was founded to prosecute an unfinished war for Irish independence seventy years earlier. During the Troubles, it grew with the aim of protecting its community from violence by the other side and the security forces. Loyalist paramilitary groups developed out of the same rationale – to protect its community from violence, especially from the IRA. They acquired weapons and recruited young men and women to use them. They formed units in different districts, towns and cities; they set up command structures, with sophisticated communications, including codes and passwords. Initially, their communities welcomed this and felt safer as a result. Then things began to change. The firepower and organisation of the IRA, and the opposition of people in Republican areas, was such that the RUC could no longer operate in them. Only the army could go in, highly armed and protecting one another. Areas fell under the de facto control of the paramilitary groups. This enabled them to force businesses to pay "protection money" to prevent them becoming targets of bombing or robberies themselves and "to support the cause". So, when I cycled past chemists, grocery stores and betting shops in the Falls Road and other Republican areas, I assumed that they had to pay such money to be allowed to stay open. Most lucrative were pubs and night clubs, where people went for entertainment, to escape the permanent tension. Residents told me that some were owned or operated by the IRA itself. Some "customers" were happy to be "protected". In some cases, businesses were financially bled dry by intimidation. In bars and clubs, customers could drink, sing and dance and let their hair down, in the knowledge that armed men were protecting the location. The members of my choir in Andersonstown chose not to invite me to the local pubs, as people in the rest of Ireland would have done. This was a wise move; any outsider in these shebeens was suspect, especially one with such a bad accent as mine.

In many areas, shops had closed and their owners had left; they did not want to operate under such intimidation. This meant better trade for the businesses that remained – many residents were afraid to go shopping or have a meal or a drink outside their own area, especially after dark. Once I went into a Chinese restaurant in a "green" district. It only offered takeaway food, one way to reduce risk. The walls were painted green, white and orange, the colours of the Irish flag. What a prudent decision, I thought. When the waiter took my order, I asked why he had chosen those colours. Smiling, he kept silent. I did not dare to ask if he paid protection money.

The construction business was a major source of income for the paramilitaries. Each year the government spent millions of pounds to build new homes and repair old ones, especially in working class areas with little or no private investment. Construction firms were vulnerable to pressure on their workers and potential attacks on their projects and their equipment. In some places, the IRA controlled allocation of housing and contracts for building and repairs. The media reported allegations that the IRA had siphoned off millions of pounds of government money that should have been spent on repairing houses in Catholic areas. In one case, the government paid out 20,000 pounds each for the repair of five three-bedroom apartments, when the repair cost elsewhere in the city for same job was less than half that. Estimates in the media put the revenue of paramilitaries from protection at between 10 million and 30 million pounds a year. The absence of state authority also enabled the paramilitaries to expand into other operations – gambling, buying and selling drugs, security companies, distribution of fake and contraband goods and smuggling, especially across the border; they channeled some of their earnings into legitimate businesses like insurance and buying property.

The situation should have been different in Loyalist areas, where the RUC was able to operate; the paramilitaries said they were working to support the RUC. But they ran rackets similar to those in the Republican areas. Both sets of paramilitaries came to resemble the Mafia in the United States and other countries; they used money from criminal activities to establish businesses in the legal economy. In a report in February 1988, *The Chicago Tribune* quoted a senior Northern Ireland police officer as saying, "It is incredible what has evolved over the last 19 years in racketeering and extortion. Both sides have lost sight of the objective for which they were created." Gordon Mahwhinney, deputy leader of the centrist Alliance Party, told the paper: "the rackets have become the major activity of these organisations."

The newspaper quoted police as saying that, of its earnings from protection, the IRA used 80 per cent "for the cause" – to buy arms and help the families of those in prison and 20 per cent for personal use. They said that, in the Loyalist paramilitaries, only 20-30 per cent of earnings went "to the cause". The rest went for the personal benefit of the members, especially the leaders, for expensive homes and cars, tailor-made suits and foreign holidays.

The victims of these rackets were the people who lived in areas in which the paramilitary organisations were powerful – in other words those whom they had been founded to protect in the first place. The residents of working class Loyalist and Republican areas feared not only violence from the opposite side but also their own. The paramilitaries were willing to kill or maim those who disobeyed them; their methods included brutal knee cappings. Initially, the residents of each side supported their political aims. But, in time, they found that they themselves had become prisoners of the paramilitaries.

The Troubles facilitated many kinds of fraud. In parts of Northern Ireland, the government's writ did not run. This opened ways to steal money from the state. Here is one small example.

My housemate Billy worked in a factory that bottled soft drinks. One Thursday afternoon I found him at home in a T-shirt drinking beer.

"Should you not be at work?" I said.

"You still do not get it yet, do you, Mark?" he said. "This afternoon I am collecting the brew (unemployment benefit), like the rest of my colleagues." The name "brew" came from the old name of the "unemployment bureau".

"But you all have jobs."

Billy laughed loudly. "So naïve! My factory is in a paramilitary area. Government inspectors do not dare to go there and nobody knows if we have a job or not. So we collect the brew, in addition to our pay."

Everybody knew that, if reluctantly, the British government was committed to maintaining Northern Ireland as it was, unless and until a majority of its people voted to join the Republic. That meant paying a enormous subsidy every year to cover the gap between what the N.I. government earned through taxes and what it spent on security, social welfare, wages for civil servants and so on. The UK government could not monitor these payments in Northern Ireland in the same way as it did in the rest of the country. This opened the way for fake applications, fake receipts and other kinds of fraud.

In the end, Billy was caught out. His boss found him mending his Mini car when he was supposed to be sick. He lost his job; he went to work for a city estate agent.

Loss assessors were not the only group who prospered in the Kafkaesque world created by the Troubles. Another were the 730 lawyers, as I wrote in a report in April 1978.

After the Troubles began in 1969, litigation work mushroomed; 10 law firms set out to get "terrorist" work. Four of the 10 were founded after 1969, one by a man interned without trial by the government. Queen's University turned out nearly twice as many law graduates in 1977 as it did in 1968. Members of one Protestant paramilitary gang carried the name of their solicitor in their wallet in case they got caught. Some police officers earned extra money by tipping off a firm after they have arrested a man. The law firms met the new demand by switching to 24-hour availability.

'One night I was woken at one in the morning and I was up till five,' one solicitor told me. 'That's not uncommon. It is one reason why the more sedate office won't handle terrorist work at all. They don't want that kind of client.'

This solicitor had spent three hours every Sunday for the last six years visiting clients in prison. The urgency came from the relatives' fear of police brutality against which, most people believed, the only defence was the presence, in person or over the phone, of a lawyer.

My article wrote: "As jurors were intimidated, judges have sat alone since 1973. The police case is normally a statement from the accused and forensic evidence. And the defence is that the statement was obtained under duress and is therefore inadmissible. Cases have become routine and quick. A murder can be dealt with in a couple of days. The conviction rate is high: less than a dozen cases have been dismissed on grounds of inadmissibility. In 1977, 1,308 people were charged with serious offences. The defending lawyer's job is made harder by the fact that many accused, usually Republicans, refuse to recognise the court, as being part of a British rule they deny. This means they dismiss their counsel, often on the morning of the trial, and offer no defence. This makes conviction and a stiffer sentence more likely. Plea bargaining is common; the accused agrees to plead guilty to a charge less serious that the original one. This gets the business over within a morning, gives the accused a lighter sentence than if he had been found guilty on the original crime and gives the police another successful conviction.

"In a murder trial, a counsel of three years' experience earns a brief fee of 500 pounds, plus 100 pounds a day from the second day onwards. A three-week murder trial earns him nearly 2,000 pounds. The 23 senior men earn between 25,000 and 60,000 pounds a year; one earned over 50,000 pounds for one four-month trial alone. Nearly all of this spending is at the public's expense, as few of those charged can pay their own legal bills; the costs are met by the state's legal aid system. By the last available figure in 1976, that cost was 602,000 pounds, 13 times what it was in 1969."

These judge-only courts were introduced in 1973. They were known as Diplock Courts, after Lord Diplock who wrote the report to the British Parliament recommending that they be set up. They heard cases involving political and terrorism-related offences; they did not have juries because its members could be subject to threats and intimidation by associates of the accused. They mainly tried Loyalist and Republican paramilitaries. The number of cases heard in Diplock courts peaked at 329 a year in the mid-1980s. After the Good Friday Agreement in 1998, the number fell to 60 a year in the mid-2000s. The British government abolished them in July 2007, a sign of how things in Northern Ireland had returned to normal.

During my time, the justice system was highly charged. Everyone in the courtroom was a potential target—judges, lawyers, policemen, witnesses and accused. During the 1970s and 1980s, the IRA killed at least five judges, as well as the wife of one and the daughter of another. The cases largely turned on confessions. The paramilitary organisations frequently accused the police of torture and inhumane treatment to obtain such confessions. Trying to maintain a system of justice during a civil war was a complex, challenging and dangerous task.

Belfast people used humour to deal with the daily stress of life. The number of stories they invented was so numerous that I cannot remember all of them. Here are a few:

One: Billy became bored of watching television at home every evening and yearned to go to a real cinema. So he plucked up the courage and, after work, went to see a film at a cinema in downtown Belfast: not many in the audience, but he greatly enjoyed it. After buying fish and chips at a takeaway, he took a bus back to his district and ate his dinner on the way: almost no-one on the bus. From the stop, it was a ten-minute walk to his house. He went briskly. The streets were empty and silent except for the sirens of the police cars and the click-clack of the steel boots of British squaddies patrolling on the pavement. With great relief, he reached his front door and took out the key. Suddenly, he felt a sharp object at the base of his spine.

"Protestant or Catholic?" said the voice. Knowing that his life depended on his answer, Billy thought for a long time.

"Jewish."

"Sorry, Billy, this is the only Palestinian in Ulster."

Two: Mary, 18, walked nervously into the church. She was trembling and did not want to go to confession; but she knew she must. Finally, she reached the confession box and knelt down. Through the wooden screen, the priest could sense her unease.

"What is it you wish to confess, my dear?"

"Father, I am so ashamed, I do not know how to say it."

"Don't be nervous. God knows all our sins. Confess and we can give you a penance."

After waiting several minutes, Mary plucked up her courage.

"Father, I have become a pro ..., a pro...," she stuttered. "I have become a pro ... a prostitute."

"What a relief. I thought you were going to say Protestant."

Three: the chairman of shipbuilder Harland and Wolff was sitting in his office, with two young men in chairs in front of his desk. They had come for a job interview.

"In the old days, we only employed Protestants," he said. "But now, with the new civil rights laws, we are open to everyone. You are both very talented candidates. I will ask each of you one question and then we decide who gets the position. James (a Protestant), in the Bible, Jesus feeds a large number of people. How many were there?"

"Five thousand," said James with a smile.

The chairman turned to the other man and said: "Sean (a Catholic), what were their names and addresses?"

Four: Dr Hamilton was driving to work at his hospital and stopped at a red light. A man with a gun forced open the door and said: "We need the car."

Helpless, the doctor had to let two men carrying a bag with a heavy object into the car. One took over the wheel and drove quickly. The road had speed bumps to slow cars down. The heart of Dr Hamilton was in his mouth as they approached the next bump. The car shook—but nothing happened. "Please drive more slowly," the doctor said. "At the next bump, something may go off." The gunman replied:

"Don't worry, we have another device in the boot."

The Reverend Jack Weir with a photograph of his father.

6

CHURCHES

ONE OF THE first things to impress me on arrival was the number of churches, of all kinds, and religious belief much stronger than in England. Belfast was covered with churches of all denominations – Presbyterian, Anglican, Catholic, Methodists, other Protestant denominations and independent mission halls. On Sunday mornings, the bells pealed out and families walked purposefully towards their churches, the men in their best suits and women wearing neat and well-chosen hats. In many districts of the city, and all over Ireland, the church was the dominant building. All this was evidence of a level of religious observance no longer found in most countries of Europe. According to the 1971 census, the largest religion in Northern Ireland was Roman Catholicism with 478,000 believers, 31.4 per cent of the population; next was Presbyterianism, the church of Grandfather, with 406,000, 26.7 per cent of the population. The census found an astonishing 101 denominations, of which sixty had over ten adherents. Most were Protestant, including four which had split from the Presbyterian church. One, the Non-Subscribing Presbyterian Church, had 596 members. The Presbyterian Church was an important part of my family's history. Grandfather had chosen to become a minister, and in 1936, he was elected to the church's highest position, Moderator. It still honoured him, especially those who had, like him, served in Manchuria. My father, on the other hand, was not religious and did not attend church. At my schools, I had attended religious services, which were compulsory; I much enjoyed the singing but was not so touched by the faith. So the intensity of belief I found in Northern Ireland was new and striking.

One result of this strong observance was the high status enjoyed by ministers and priests, as leaders and spokesmen of their communities. The government and political leaders consulted them on public issues and listened to what they said. The saddest thing in this most religious part of Britain was the inability of the churches to stop the violence. It was not for want of trying. From the pulpits and in speeches and newspaper and magazine articles, the ministers and priests appealed constantly to their congregations not to kill, injure and bomb; they asked them to settle their differences through peaceful means. As I described in the story of the Reverend Jack Weir, many were involved in peace-making efforts, at risk to their personal safety and their reputations in their own communities. But the paramilitaries on both sides did not listen. This led me to conclude that the conflict was tribal, more than religious.

A man described himself as Protestant not because he attended a Methodist or Anglican church every Sunday but because he was born into that community and belonged to it. This became clear when I talked to residents of the Shankill Road and those close to the Loyalist paramilitaries. Few attended church or had any religious belief; but they were fervent "Protestants" in wanting to retain the British status of Northern Ireland. If I questioned the morality of attacking members of the other community, they replied they were simply responding to the violence of the IRA and other Republican groups, whose aggression left them no choice. Over decades after the 1950s, the mainstream Protestant churches lost contact with many urban working class Protestants in Belfast. With the onset of the Troubles, there was a significant shift of population into "safe" areas. Many Protestant church buildings in the central urban areas of Belfast had closed.

During my time in Belfast, the most conspicuous minister was Reverend Ian Paisley. In 1946, he became an evangelist minister and, in 1951, co-founded the Free Presbyterian Church. He was never a member of my grandfather's Presbyterian Church in Ireland (PCI). According to the 1971 census, his church had 7,337 members; by the 1991 census, the number had risen to 12,000, less than one per cent of the Northern Ireland population. His unfulfilled aspiration was to split the PCI as he had weakened and divided the Ulster Unionist Party. While his religious influence was limited, he was an important political figure. In 1970, he became a Member of Parliament for North Antrim; in the following year, he founded the Democratic Unionist Party (DUP).

To understand Paisley better, I went to a Sunday morning service at his large Martyrs Memorial Church on the Ravenhill Road in Belfast, which it overlooks the spacious Ormeau Park. As befits an evangelical, fundamentalist church, there were no religious pictures or imagery. Several hundred seats faced a wall, with the pulpit in the centre. When Dr. Paisley mounted the pulpit, there was awe and excitement; most of the seats were full. His sermon was like nothing I had heard before—criticising the Catholic church and the Pope and including an extensive commentary on political events in Ireland. He said that the Irish Republic was a country controlled by the Catholic hierarchy. He called the European Union a conspiracy to create a Roman Catholic super-state controlled by the Vatican. It was a mixture of religion and politics. A talented orator, he held the audience at his fingertips for sixty minutes. He was charismatic and had a good sense of humour. You could not hear such a sermon in any other church in Europe. It was hard to believe these were the words of a minister of religion. When friends, especially journalists, came to visit me, I took them to the Martyrs Memorial as a quick way to understand the Troubles.

During my three and a half years there, Paisley was a major political figure and his DUP was on the way to becoming the largest Unionist Party. He opposed all efforts to settle the conflict through power-sharing between the two sides and to involve the Irish government in Northern affairs. In 1977, he was a leader of the United Unionist Action Council; it organised a general strike in May that year, to restore devolved government to Northern Ireland. Armed loyalist paramilitaries blocked roads and intimidated workers and attacked businesses which did not co-operate. The strike lasted only three days, because a majority of people opposed it and the security forces had prepared well in advance. Paisley himself was arrested at a roadblock and charged with obstruction of the highway. During the strike, the loyalist paramilitaries killed three people and 41 RUC officers were injured and 115 people charged with offences. Was this the work of a minister of religion?

If you ask older people in Europe about Paisley, the only thing they remember about him is a speech by Pope John Paul II on October 11, 1988 to the European Parliament in Strasbourg. A Euro MP, Paisley held up a poster reading "Pope John Paul II Antichrist". Other MEPs shouted at him; he was forcibly removed from the chamber. His behaviour shocked people all over Europe; but it was music to the ears of his supporters at home. They were the ones who elected him and went to his church.

One afternoon, I was talking to the staff in a Sinn Fein office. Everyone had had a few drinks; the atmosphere was relaxed.

"After his morning service, Ian Paisley talks to his church members in the forecourt of his church," I said. "There is a clear line of sight across the park opposite (from a Republican area). He would be an easy target. You have never thought of it?"

"Never, never," came the reply firmly. "He is our best propaganda weapon with the British public. He makes them think that all the Prods (Protestants) here are mad. Who wants to support and pay for such people?"

For many years, Paisley and his supporters organised noisy, threatening and sometimes violent protests outside the Assembly Hall of the Presbyterian Church in Ireland (PCI) on the opening night of the General Assembly, its most important event of the year. His supporters frequently telephoned PCI ministers in the middle of the night, sometimes at 3 a.m., and harassed them. They especially targetted ecumenism and contacts with the Roman Catholic Church. One object of their wrath was the Reverend Jack Withers, who in 1964 had invited a Catholic priest to give a talk to young people on the work of the Second Vatican Council that had opened two years earlier. After Paisley threatened a "monster" demonstration on the evening of the meeting at the church involved, it had to be cancelled. In her book "Jack Withers", his daughter Sheilah Bradley described what happened then.

"There began a period of persecution for Jack and the family that lasted fully six months. As Jack stated in the press, 'Our house was constantly molested by day and night … the legality of my parents' marriage was doubted and my wife's life was threatened." As a family, we were offered police protection."

This hostility culminated in a noisy demonstration by Paisley and 2,000 of his supporters outside the PCI headquarters on June 3, 1968, when Reverend Jack Withers began his appointment as Moderator of the General Assembly of the church.

"He was under constant attack for many years from the Protestant underworld," his daughter wrote. "Eventually, it did take its toll. He started having angina attacks which eventually culminated in a coronary thrombosis in the seventies. He decided to take early retirement in 1971 when he was only sixty."

"Dr No" continued to oppose everything until 2007, when he agreed to share power with Sinn Fein and become First Minister of Northern Ireland; Sinn Fein's Martin McGuiness, a former IRA commander, became his deputy. Such an agreement – to form a joint government with the 'enemy' – was unthinkable during my time and for the next 25 years.

What if he had decided to do this in the 1970s? How many lives would have been saved? While he did not pull the trigger, those who did took inspiration from his words. While a political leader must listen to his supporters, someone as charismatic and persuasive as Paisley had a great influence over them. History will remember him as a political, as well as a religious, leader. His decision toward the end of his life to share power with Sinn Fein and Martin McGuiness cost him dearly. He was dismissed as the minister of the Martyrs Memorial Church and ceased to be the Moderator of the Free Presbyterian Church. After he passed away in September 2014, I asked a minister friend in Belfast for his judgement.

"Better to be converted late in life than never be converted at all," he said. "Past behaviour does not always close off future possibilities, even when there has been no repentance for the past."

I was able to learn about my grandfather's church from Rev Jack Weir and other ministers I met. The Presbyterians began to arrive in Northern Ireland in the early 1600s from Scotland; they were encouraged to settle by the British government which wanted a large population of English-speaking Protestants. They settled on land that had been taken from the Gaelic chieftains; they cultivated it, cleared forests and built towns. The first presbytery was formed at Carrickfergus in 1642; that is the date which the church regards as its foundation in Ireland. This settlement was not peaceful. The Gaelic Irish had lost their land but remained as tenants and labourers. They launched rebellions, which were ruthlessly suppressed by the British army. No quarter was given on either side. This remained part of the folk memory of both sides during the Troubles. By 1659, the number of Presbyterians in Ulster had reached 33,000. Many also came in the 1690s due to a famine in Scotland. After the "Glorious Revolution" of 1688 which established the Protestant William and Mary on the British throne with limited powers, and the Battle of the Boyne in Ireland two years later, there were more opportunities for Protestants to settle in Ireland.

After the British consolidated their rule of Ireland from the late 17th century, they established three classes. Top were Anglicans who belonged to the established Church of England. The landowners, the leaders of the military, police, government, business and education belonged to this class. Second were the Presbyterians and other non-Anglican Protestants; they were not allowed to work in the government or hold official positions. Presbyterian marriages were not fully and legally recognised until 1845. The third class, the majority, was Catholic; under the Penal Laws, they were subject to even more restrictions. So it is not surprising that, to escape these inequalities, up to 250,000 Presbyterians from Ireland and Scotland emigrated to the United States during the 18th century. Another factor was the Irish Famine of 1740-41, which is estimated to have killed between 13 and 20 per cent of the population of 2.4 million. Many Presbyterians were active as Scots Irish in the U.S. revolutionary army and movement that defeated the British army and formed the first state to win independence from the British Empire anywhere in the world. Up to ten U.S. Presidents are of Scots-Irish descent—a fact ignored by most Irish Americans who consider President John F. Kennedy as the first President with Irish roots.

This mass migration preceded by a century the better known migration of tens of thousands of Irish Catholics after the Great Famine of the 1840s. Inspired by the American and French revolutions, a group of Presbyterians in Belfast set up the Society of United Irishmen in 1791, together with Catholics and other "dissenters". When the British refused their demands for reform, they launched an armed rebellion in 1798. The British army suppressed the rebellion with great cruelty; the final death toll was between 10,000 and 30,000. Many leaders of the rebellion were Presbyterian, mainly from Belfast and Counties Antrim and Down. What was new to me in this history was the fact that many Irish Protestants had made common cause with their Catholic neighbours for a fairer and more equal society and an end to the privileges of the ruling Anglican class. Irish Republicanism was not exclusive to the Catholics, as I had previously thought.

But this changed during the 19th century. The 1798 rebellion was a serious warning to the British establishment. In 1800, the Parliaments of Great Britain and Ireland voted to set up a single Parliament in London under the Acts of Unions. Ireland lost its own Parliament and its MPs went to sit in Parliament. The British government decided this was the best way to control Ireland and prevent moves toward self-rule or independence. To ensure its rule in Ireland, it had to bind the Presbyterians and members of other Protestant denominations to the Unionist side. It was greatly helped in this by Cardinal Paul Cullen, Catholic primate of Ireland from 1852 to 1878. Deeply conservative, he 'romanised' the church and was fervently anti-Protestant. "Error has no rights," he said.

Cardinal Cullen strongly promoted Catholic religious education and he left a deep legacy. During my time, the vast majority of Catholics in Northern Ireland went to church schools, while Protestants attended state or private schools, which were largely Protestant. Little has changed since then. Government figures published in 2019 found that 1.3 per cent of pupils in Catholic grammar schools were Protestant, while only about 12 per cent of Catholics attend non-denominational, state grammar schools.

In 1976, ACT (All Children Together) published a paper with proposals for shared management of schools in Northern Ireland. This paper comprised an early model for integrating existing schools and the development of a curriculum to promote "a common pattern of religious and moral education, and of historical and cultural studies." In 1978, the Education (N.I.) Act encapsulated the ACT proposals. Unfortunately, the main Christian churches did not respond to the facility offered for shared management of schools.

In 1981, the first planned, integrated school, Lagan College, was established. This is what the school says of its mission on its website: "Lagan College was founded in 1981 as a religious response to the challenge of community conflict and a religiously divided school system in Northern Ireland. Since 1974, the All Children Together Movement (ACT) had been lobbying the Churches and the Government to take the initiative in educating Protestant and Catholic children together. Religious segregation of school children was almost complete. Practically all Catholic children attended Catholic schools. State schools were de facto Protestant. ACT argued that one of the most powerful responses which Christians could give to the charge that the fighting was about religion would be for Protestants and Catholics to educate their children together in the same schools."

Today Lagan College has 1,262 students, up from 28 in 1981. By 1987, there were seven such new integrated schools and, by

2019, 65.

In August 1907, the Vatican issued the decree Ne Temere (Not Rashly); it required written undertakings that children of Protestant-Catholic marriages be raised as Catholic. Previously, the custom was for the sons of such marriages to go to the father's church and the daughters to the mother's. The Irish clergy enthusiastically applied this decree; as a result, the Protestant population of the Irish Republic fell dramatically, up to 80 per cent. The church Cullen created was triumphal and exclusive. The Protestants of Ireland feared that an independent state would have Catholicism as its official religion, at their expense, so the vast majority, including the Presbyterians, opposed it. From this fear came the slogan "Home Rule means Rome Rule", which Paisley delighted in saying. By the end of the 19th century, in Northern Ireland, Nationalism meant Catholic and Unionism meant Protestant. Since Partition in 1922, both parts of Ireland have been dominated by the exclusive and excluding ideologies of Irish Catholic National and Ulster Protestant Unionism, which have been described as "me as not you". It is "oppositional identity"—"anti-Britishness" in Irish identity is matched by "anti-Catholicism" in Unionist identity.

So it remained during my time in Belfast. By 1900, the number of Presbyterians in Ireland reached 642,000, a historic high. Now the church has a membership of about 225,000 people in 536 congregations in 403 churches all over Ireland; about 96 per cent of the membership is in Northern Ireland. This reduction is due to secularism and the exodus of third-level students to study in Britain, from where most do not return.

During my time, I often met Presbyterian ministers, usually on sad occasions—after an attack on one of their church members. I greatly respected them for having to care for the grief and traumatism of the family. The best exposition I have read of their position is in the book *A Precarious Belonging – Presbyterians and the Conflict in Ireland,* by Reverend John Dunlop, Moderator of the General Assembly in 1992-93. The book was published in 1995. I did not know him then but came to know him later. In the 1990s, we went on a week-long visit to Liaoning province for a documentary film on the church's missionary work there; it was the nearest I came to meeting my grandfather.

"After Partition in 1922, much was achieved materially within Northern Ireland, while at the same time relationships between north and south and between nationalists and unionists deteriorated. The border was the prior question at all times … (will Ireland be united into a single state or will Northern Ireland continue to part of the United Kingdom?) … It would be difficult to imagine two groups of people living so close together and failing so completely either to understand or to accommodate one another," he wrote. After the Troubles started, militants from both sides fanned the flames of hatred. "Those people who resisted necessary reform and those who fomented discord in a volatile situation carry a heavy weight of responsibility for detonating 25 years of mayhem. People who chose not to handle the volatile and explosive situation with care put themselves and thousands of others at risk ... The whole community failed, in 1968 and thereafter, to come together to understand one another and to address the outstanding issues together."

The book also describes his experiences during the Troubles.

"Not only was it my responsibility to conduct the funerals of some of the people murdered by the IRA. I was also conscious of the deep wells of grief within families and congregations which had seen the people they love prematurely laid to rest, often in the quiet churchyards beside the buildings where they worship Sunday by Sunday. People have often felt isolated and vulnerable … It is difficult to report grief in such a way that it can be understood by people who are not grieving ... In ways which can only be experienced from within a community, carrying as it does its tribal nightmares, it is difficult to imagine how every murder shook the Protestant community like a tremor, particularly those communities in isolated areas around the border. The same can clearly be said about the effect of loyalist killings on, say, the Catholics of north Belfast."

The result of these attacks was a migration of Protestants from Belfast city to the satellite towns around it and from border districts to safer areas.

"One of the things that has kept Northern Ireland from descending into total chaos has been the willingness of bereaved people to forgive those who killed the people they love, and the stated desire of them, and many others, that there should be no revenge," he wrote. "Forgiveness is not easy. The very possibility of forgiveness cost God the price of Christ's death. It is from that agony that the generosity of God's forgiveness proceeds. It is that which opens up a new future without denying the reality of the past."

I found Reverend Dunlop's book most instructive in explaining the work and thinking of ministers during the Troubles. These are not issues that can be easily discussed. I found it hard to ask ministers and priests: what do you say to the widow of a policeman or civilian who has been killed? How do you deal with the hatred and desire for revenge?

"It was frequently the bereaved people who asked that there should be no revenge," said Reverend John Dunlop. "It was comforting for bereaved and desolate people to know that people stood with them in their grief, without people actually being able to fully comprehend the depths of their loss. The Christian faith affirms that Jesus plumbed the depths of injustice and violence in his death and, in his resurrection, opened a future on the other side of death."

He referred me to a speech he gave in February 1998 to the Centre of Theology and Public Issues at New College in Edinburgh University. "That different parts of the Northern Ireland community have not descended into the atrocities of civil war says something significant about their forbearance and their capacity to absorb suffering ... Consider what would have happened if the resources of the churches had been deployed in the service of vengeance. By condemning violence, calling for no retaliation and encouraging forgiveness, the churches and many individuals have ensured that the conflict in Ireland has been contained to some degree. The underlying issues have not, however, been resolved."

I am most grateful to Rev Dunlop for his friendship and his writings. Better than anyone else, he gave me an insight into the church of which Grandfather was a minister and the character of its ministers. He has been the closest I came to meeting Grandfather. He died in 1952 in Belfast; I never had the opportunity to meet him.

The Catholic priest most helpful to me was Father Des Wilson, whom I mentioned in Chapter One. Born in July 1925, he grew up above his father's public house in Belfast city centre and in a house in the suburbs. In April and May 1941, the Germans bombed the city, killing nearly 1,000 people. The suffering he saw was one factor that persuaded him to become a priest. He had a comfortable middle-class life until he moved to Ballymurphy in west Belfast in 1966. This was a district of 600 pre-fabricated concrete council houses built by the post-war government in 1947 to meet demand from the rising population.

Before 1968, many such public housing estates included both Protestants and Catholics. But, after 1968, people segregated themselves, voluntarily or through intimidation. So the residents of Ballymurphy came to belong to only one 'tribe'—Catholic. Father Wilson was shocked by the poverty, low quality of housing and abuse against women he saw. Offered a comfortable parish house, he instead chose to live in a terraced house on the estate, next to his parishioners. The outbreak of the Troubles in 1969 exacerbated the district's unemployment, drug abuse, alcoholism and violence. By the mid-1970s, the estate had 20,000 people and unemployment of over 30 per cent. There were few areas for play and recreation; there was litter and broken glass everywhere. The IRA was active; it was an ideal place to recruit young men who had few prospects of a stable job or income or a future outside the Nationalist enclaves. The Troubles had exacerbated this sense of isolation.

In 1971, Father Wilson took the extraordinary step of inviting Mother Teresa, probably the most famous Catholic nun in the world, to come to Ballymurphy. In October that year, she and four other members of her Sisters of Charity Order moved into a house in 123 Springhill Avenue. At this time of deep misery and suffering, the residents warmly welcomed the nuns who had come from so far away to help. But, after only 18 months, the five sisters left suddenly. The church's explanation is that Mother Teresa left of her own free will. But many residents believed the parish priest did not welcome outside missionaries coming to Belfast; he preferred local people. In any event, relations between Father Wilson and his superiors were deteriorating. In 1975, he resigned. He was forbidden to say Mass in a church and was no longer being paid. He lived off savings, writing, broadcasting and lecturing and help from Presbyterian and Quaker friends. He continued to live in Ballymurphy and said Mass in his house.

For an outsider like myself, the open invitation to his house was invaluable. Because he was not part of the church hierarchy, he was a free agent and more able to express his opinions. He was popular among Ballymurphy residents; his house was always full of visitors. His invitation was also a protection from anyone who asked what this strange man, like me, with a Brit accent was doing there. It was a precious opportunity to talk to people in the area about their lives, their children and their aspirations.

How could the IRA establish such power in these Catholic neighbourhoods where they planned their operations? My conclusion was that most people felt trapped. Like the IRA, they detested the British Army, the RUC and the Protestant establishment that had run Northern Ireland since 1922. But they were also terrified of the IRA and its ability to kill and injure people, including those on the Catholic side, and cause destruction that crippled the economy. They feared that their children would join the organisation. But they did not dare to oppose it. So they were victims twice over.

Father Wilson stepped forward to confront these dangerous challenges. With another priest, he worked to end blood feuds between different Republican factions. They also began a dialogue with loyalist paramilitaries. His priest's collar largely gave him immunity, but it was not absolute. An individual gunman on one side or the other might have chosen to attack him. To help the residents, he set up the Conway Education Centre; lack of qualifications was the biggest handicap to leaving the ghetto and joining mainstream society. By the 1980s, his home had become too small for the many classes he organised. They moved to a disused mill and offered vocational and non-vocational courses to hundreds of students. He established projects to provide employment in the area. By the mid-1980s, his relationship with the Diocese of Down and Connor was re-established; he was allowed to continue his ministry. In total, he lived in the Ballymurphy estate for half a century.

He passed away in November 2019. Father Joe McVeigh, a

personal friend, gave the homily at his funeral in Belfast: "He was in the tradition of prophets through the ages, sharing their passion for truth and justice. He was a humble man, never seeking the limelight for himself but only to show solidarity with the oppressed and the downtrodden. Des probably did not see himself as a prophet. He sometimes described himself as a 'mischief maker'," he said.

I thank Father Wilson very much for opening his door and allowing me to learn something of the complex and dangerous world in which he lived.

In most parts of Europe, "mixed marriage" means a union between a white and a black person, people of different races. In Northern Ireland, it meant a marriage between a Protestant and Catholic. With the society so divided, such a marriage was extremely difficult. Usually, both families opposed it. In which church should the marriage be held? Where should the couple live? What religion should the children follow? Sometimes such couples had to move to mainland Britain for the marriage and live there in order to avoid all these complications. In any event, it was a sensitive subject and one worth writing about. So I was delighted to be invited to a weekend at a Catholic retreat in County Fermanagh to meet couples of these marriages and learn how they were dealing with these difficulties.

The venue was deep in the countryside, surrounded by trees, fields and birds, a pleasant change from the harsh urban landscape of Belfast, with its "Peace Walls", barbed wire fences, road blocks and graffiti. Our host was a handsome priest in his early forties, with blonde hair and full of energy. He ably chaired the sessions, during which the couples described their experiences with their families, daily life and work and the hostility they faced from relatives or neighbours. For me, it was "off the record"; this meant that I could use the material but not mention anyone by name nor give information that would disclose where they lived. It was moving and informative. After dinner on the Saturday evening, everyone went to bed except for the priest and me. He invited me into his large study; the walls were covered by books.

"How well read you are," I said.

"Not quite," he said with a smile. Several shelves of 'books' turned out to be cabinets full of alcohol. He liberally dispensed whisky ad our tongues loosened after the disciplined dialogue of the afternoon.

He said that he spent about half of the year working in the United States. It is free-er and more relaxing to live in a large anonymous city, where few people know who you are, he said; in small communities in Ireland, there are eyes everywhere and it is hard to stray, especially if you are a priest. He told me about a girlfriend he had in the U.S. I was not familiar enough with the Catholic church to know if this was normal or whether he was simply telling a good story to impress a visitor. Men often boast about their income and sexual conquests. The time passed quickly enough. The next morning there was Mass and more sessions with the couples, so it was time for sleep. He showed me to my small room, equipped with a bed, a washing basin and a window. The building was dark and completely quiet; everyone else was asleep. I thanked him for his hospitality and noticed that he had remained in the room and shut the door behind him. What happens now? I thought to myself. Does he want a sexual encounter?

"No, thanks," I said firmly.

The priest was shorter than I but well-built and stronger. He thought for a moment, then turned and left the room. The next morning I rose early and shared breakfast with the visitors—so courteous and friendly. Then we stood in the corridor and watched the priest, in his spotless white cassock, come down the stairs for the morning Mass. He smiled broadly at everyone, including me. Nothing had happened.

My grandparents in front of their house in Faku, northeast China.

7

Clan Chief in Setubal

The location was a large vineyard in Setubal, a port fifty kilometres south of Lisbon. On a terrace overlooking the vineyard, I was sipping red wine with Jorge O'Neill, head of the Clanaboy O'Neills. He was recounting the extraordinary history of his family and how a descendant of the King of Ireland became a rich businessman and maker of wine in southern Portugal. This visit enabled me to learn, for the first time, the story of my distinguished ancestors.

The exile of Jorge's family began on September 14 1607, when Hugh O'Neill, Earl of Tyrone, and 98 of his family and retainers left Rathmullan on Lough Swilly in County Donegal for Europe. He was the last inaugurated King of Ulster and never returned to Ireland. This came to be known as the "Flight of the Earls" and marked the end of the Gaelic aristocracy in the north of Ireland. His lands were given to Protestant settlers from Scotland and England; the Ulster Plantation had begun. It was a milestone in the nation's history.

Hugh was descended from Niall Noigiallach, Niall of the Nine Hostages, an Irish king of the fourth century A.D. The O'Neills were high kings of Ireland for over 600 years and dominated the northern half of Ireland, before the English conquest that began in the 12th century. While the English king was the formal sovereign, the O'Neills retained much of their lands and power.

Born in 1550, Hugh O'Neill had a complex political career, often working with the English. But, in 1598, he turned against them. On August 14 that year, his troops destroyed an English army of 4,000 men at the battle of the Yellow Ford in County Armagh and killed its commander; it was the greatest defeat of English arms in Ireland. In October 1601, a Spanish army arrived in Kinsale, County Cork, in the far south, to help Hugh O'Neill; but it was defeated by the British forces. Queen Elizabeth I sent Lord Mountjoy as a new Lord Lieutentant of Ireland, together with 16,000 troops and 1,500 horses. In 1603, he defeated Hugh O'Neill; he was made to kneel for several hours in submission. Mountjoy smashed the O'Neill coronation stone at Tullaghoge, between Dungannon and Cookstown, the symbol of his power. Hugh O'Neill was the last clan chief who might have defeated the English monarch; his flight meant the English victory in Ireland.

As Jorge told it, Hugh was a blessed migrant. Over the centuries, tens of thousands of people have left Ireland in poverty and hardship to make a new life in Britain and the Americas. But Hugh belonged to the European nobility; he was welcomed by the Catholic kings of France, Spain and Portugal. Hugh himself died of fever in Rome on July 20, 1616. After their arrival in Portugal, the O'Neills married into the local aristocracy and bought vineyards. Their children also married into the upper class. Jorge himself was a wealthy man; he was chairman of one of the largest private businesses in the country, with 15 factories and 2,000 workers in Portugal and Africa. After the Carnation Revolution of 1974, the new left-wing government nationalised many banks and large business; the state came to own up to two-thirds of national GNP.

"We were fortunate," Jorge said. "Ours was a medium-size enterprise and for that reason avoided nationalisation. We had to have an exit plan, of course, so we bought a property near Ballymena (Co Antrim, Northern Ireland)."

The family owned the sprawling vineyard where we were sitting. What a different story from that of the thousands of Irish people who arrived in Boston, Liverpool and Glasgow with nothing and faced poverty and discrimination. Jorge sent his daughters to be educated at an Irish Dominican convent founded in 1639 in Belem, Lisbon. Many Irish nuns in the 17th century, mainly from gentry families, emigrated to join convents in Flanders, France, Spain and Portugal. Several convents were supported by the royal families and nobility of Europe.

Jorge spoke five languages and had a large library full of philosophical works. This included three letters to his grandfather Hugo from Sir Roger Casement, dated just before the British executed him in 1916 for trying to smuggle arms into Ireland from a German U-boat. One was a thank-you letter that might have been written in gratitude for funds which his grandfather perhaps sent to the Republican cause. He donated one of the letters to the National Library in Dublin.

In 1973, at the age of 64, Jorge paid his first visit to his ancestral place, taking his daughter to a convent summer school and visiting Dublin and Belfast. In June 1982, with his Italian-born wife and twenty Portuguese kinsmen, Jorge went to Shane's Castle, County Antrim. He was enthroned a chief of his branch of the clan, in the first such ceremony in 400 years. The Chief Herald of Ireland recognised him as head of the Clanaboy branch of the O'Neill family. His host at Shane's Castle was Lord Raymond O'Neill, head of the family's Protestant line and nephew of Lord Terence O'Neill of the Maine, who served as Premier of Northern Ireland from 1963 to 1969. In this family, fortunately, there were no disputes between the Protestant and Catholic lines. The enthronement attracted members of the clan from America, Canada, France, Spain, West Germany, Australia, New Zealand, England and Scotland and the Republic.

Lord Raymond Arthur Clanaboy O'Neill was born in 1933 and became Baron O'Neill in 1944 after the death of his father in action in Italy during World War Two. He was educated at Eton and the Royal Agricultural College. He had a distinguished career in the British army; he also held public offices in Northern Ireland, including chairman of the N.I. Tourist Board from 1975 to 1980. In 1922, the IRA burnt down the castle, but the family rebuilt it. Lord O'Neill remained there throughout the Troubles, farming the land. Today his eldest son Shane is responsible for the day-to-day running of the 3,500 acres of farmland. The castle is a working estate and has hosted scout jamborees, dance events, the Game Fair and Antrim Show; the Game of Thrones has used its grounds as a film location. Lord O'Neill is a railway enthusiast and an avid collector of railway memorabilia. Each year the castle hosts the May Day Steam Rally – it used to have its own railway.

Some things, however, remained unclear. From my observation, most O'Neills in Ireland were Catholic, and only a minority – including the branch to which I belonged – were Protestant. How and why did some became Protestant? During the centuries of British rule, some Catholics converted to Anglicanism, Presbyterianism and other Protestant denominations. Some did so out of religious conviction, others to make their lives better and escape from the penal laws imposed against Catholics. At their most severe, they banned Catholics from most public offices, the army, the law and judiciary, teaching and owning a horse worth more than five pounds. In Republican areas of Belfast, I heard a perjorative term for these converts – "soupers". This referred to the Great Famine of the 1840s; the only food available for many people was soup distributed by large landowners. "When the starving peasant reached the front of the queue, he declared himself a Protestant to ensure he was given a bowl of soup," was how one lady explained it. "The term 'souper' came to mean those who converted because they could not endure the restrictions imposed on Catholics," she said. One day I raised this topic with a taxi driver in a Republican area; I asked him why some O'Neills were Protestant. "Sure, it does not matter," he said. "You are all part of our family."

After I went to live abroad, I discovered that O'Neills had emigrated to many countries, as well as Portugal. Most powerful was Thomas "Tip" O'Neill, the 47th Speaker of the U.S. House of Representatives from 1977 to 1987. That made him third in line for the presidency. If a plane carrying the President and Vice-President had crashed, an O'Neill would for a time have held the most important job in the world. He served as a Democrat representing North Boston from 1953 to 1987. Another prominent American was Paul O'Neill, chairman and CEO of industrial giant Alcoa and chairman of the Rand Corporation. He served as Secretary of the Treasury from January 2001 to December 2002, under President George W. Bush. The most famous member of the clan in the United States was playwright Eugene Gladstone O'Neill, who won the Nobel Prize for Literature in 1936. His best known work was "Long Day's Journey into Night". Like most of his work, it is a tragedy, reflecting the sad and tormented life of the author and his family. He was born in October 1888 in a hotel in New York City, the son of an Irish immigrant father who was an actor and an alcoholic. Many Americans consider Eugene O'Neill their country's most famous playwright.

Later, when I was living in China, I learnt of another prominent American member of the family. In 2002, China's best basketball player, Yao Ming, 2.3 metres tall, moved from the Shanghai Sharks team to the Houston Rockets. The matches of the Rockets in the National Basketball Association (NBA) became an instant hit on Chinese television. At that time, the top American player in the NBA was Shaquille O'Neal, 2.16 metres tall and weighing 147 kilograms, with the Los Angeles Lakers. The two giants met for the first time in a match between the Rockets and the Lakers; unfortunately for China, the Lakers won. The next morning, I was discussing the game with a schoolboy in Shanghai. I said that Shaquille was a relative of mine but wealthier and more talented. The young man looked at the newspaper photo and said: "Wait a minute, you are the wrong colour. You are joking with me. How come you have the same name?"

I did not know the history of Shaquille's family but told the boy that, after President Abraham Lincoln emancipated slaves in 1863, they took surnames. Some adopted the names of presidents, like Washington and Jackson; many took the name of their masters or whites with whom they were associated – so Shaquille's ancestor may have worked for an Irish-American. With the NBA broadcasts, Shaquille became a household name in China; he was an excellent way to break the ice in telephone conversations. Chinese officials are well trained to say nothing to foreigners; but, after five minutes of banter over "my cousin" Shaquille, they were often willing to tell you something.

Dr Hugh Gibbons and his wife, Josie.

8

The Irish Republic

For three and a half years, I lived in Belfast, capital of Northern Ireland. During this time, I made many visits to the Republic of Ireland, a journey of two hours by road or rail. These trips helped to relieve the tension of living in the Troubles and gave me the chance to explore the part of the island that had decided to leave Britain fifty years earlier. My new passport had been issued by the government in Dublin. It considered people born in the North, including Father and Grandfather, as its own citizens; that is why it was, and is, willing to give passports to their descendants. So visiting the Republic was an essential part of my journey, to understand its relationship with the North and to meet more of my fellow citizens.

Through the introduction of a friend, I was able to meet members of the Gibbons family in Dublin. They kindly invited me to visit the family home and meet their father, Dr Hugh Gibbons, a medical doctor and a TD (Teachta Dála), a member of the Irish Parliament (Dáil). He represented the counties of Roscommon and Leitrim in the northwest; he lived in the small village of Keadue, population 154, in County Roscommon. It was a journey of two and a half hours from Belfast; I set off from Belfast in the early afternoon one Friday—better not to drive through the border areas after dark. There was an excellent road, the M1, which took me to County Fermanagh, in the southwest corner of Northern Ireland, and the town of Belcoo, where you cross into the South. From there, it was 50 minutes to Keadue.

The family home was in a row of houses in the main street of the village. JoAnn, the elder daughter of Dr Gibbons, was my contact; she was at home and introduced me to her father, and mother Josie. About sixty, he was a man of medium height, of straight build, slim and with powerful eyes. They showed me into the reception room of the house. On the wall one side of the mantelpiece was a large photograph of Éamon de Valera, the most important political figure in the Republic in the 20th century; he had been President for fourteen years until his retirement in 1973 – and the one whose speeches Father had mimicked in our London dining room a dozen years earlier. This photograph told me that Dr Gibbons belonged to the Fianna Fáil party, which had been founded by de Valera and had ruled Ireland for 33 of the 53 years since independence in 1922.

At that first meeting, Dr Gibbons was polite and reserved, as befits one of the district's most prominent citizens in meeting this stranger with a Brit accent who had dropped out of the sky. But, since the visitor was a friend of his daughter, he was willing to spare the time. I asked him about his work as a TD and how he combined this with a medical practice that covered a large area of over 66 square kilometres. The Dáil met in Dublin, which was 150 kilometres and a journey of almost three hours away. It was gruelling, he said. He usually spent two-three days a week at the Dáil and the rest of the week attending to his patients; this meant the appointments ran into the weekends. Since it was a rural area, he had to drive long distances to visit patients who lived all over the district.

Dr Gibbons was a child of the new Ireland. He was born in July 1916 at Ballybeg, near Strokestown, County Roscommon, and was five years old when the country won its independence from Britain in January 1922. He had childhood memories of Black and Tan raids on his family's grocery shop and public bar, and of his father mounted as a hostage on the back of an army truck to prevent it being attacked by the local IRA. One of the county's most talented Gaelic football players, he won two All-Ireland senior finals with Roscommon in 1943 and 1944. A Dublin journalist told me once that the best qualification to enter the Dáil was to win an All-Ireland title or be the child of a winner. He was speaking only partly in jest—the finals of Gaelic football and hurling are held in front of up to 90,000 people in Croke Park in Dublin, as well as a nationwide radio and television audience; this gives the players the best public platform. Dr Gibbons served as TD for Roscommon from 1965 to 1977, being re-elected twice in 1969 and 1973. He retired to concentrate on his medical practice but continued to campaign on public issues for his native county. He and his wife Josie had four sons and two daughters.

As we talked more, his reserve disappeared; he became more animated and friendly. His family and history was rooted in Roscommon, a county of 2,550 square kilometres and 60,000 people, one of the most sparsely populated counties in Ireland. Landlocked, it relied mainly on farming and small industries in its various towns. Dr Gibbons's district, the parish of Kilronan, had in addition the Arigna Coal Mine, close to Keadue; mining began there in 1765. Dr Gibbons said that the partition of the island had been an economic disaster for counties in northwest Ireland like Roscommon.

"Before 1922, the economic centre for these counties was Belfast. Our transport links and markets were in the North," he said. "Suddenly, there was a border and we had to look to the south."

He spoke with reverence of de Valera, who founded the

Fianna Fáil party in 1926. Born in New York in October 1882, de Valera was brought to Ireland by an uncle when he was two. He grew up in County Limerick and was educated at Blackrock College in Dublin, one of the country's best known secondary schools. He started life as a teacher of mathematics. In November 1913, he signed up for the Irish volunteers and joined the political revolution. He was a commander during the Easter Rising in Dublin in 1916. After the rebels surrendered, the British sentenced de Valera to death but did not carry it out, in part because the U.S. consulate made representations for him, one of its citizens. After Independence, he served as Taoiseach (Prime Minister) for a total of sixteen years and President from 1959 to 1973.

Like de Valera, Dr Gibbons was a devout Catholic and promoter of the Irish language, which he spoke well. He did not drink or smoke. His family was most impressive. All six children received a university education – two became college professors, one a lawyer, another a judge, and another a counseling psychologist in the United States. The eldest son, Brian, became a doctor like his father but settled in Wales. He served as Labour Party Assembly member for Aberavon from May 1999 to May 2011. From 2005 to 2007, he served as Welsh government Minister for Health and Social Services and, from 2007 to 2009, Minister for Social Justice and Local Government. The children were very kind to me; we remain in touch today.

Since his patients were spread over a large area, Dr Gibbons spent a lot of time driving his Fiat car. During my later visits, he invited me to go with him. As we passed a house, he explained how many people lived there, and when the children were born in the days before hospital births had become the norm. He had a deep knowledge of the residents that was probably matched only by the local priest. Close to Keadue was Kilronan mountain whose natural resources provided the coal deposits for Arigna coal mines. A power station using the coal opened in 1958; it employed sixty people. He had many miners among his patients. There is also a notable musical heritage in the area; the famous Irish composer and harper, 'the Last of the Bards,' Turlough O'Carolan (1670-1738), lived in the district and is buried in the local churchyard. Each year, Keadue village hosts the O'Carolan Harp Festival which has attracted harpists from as far away as Japan. Thanks to these visits, I was able to understand something of life in Roscommon and the views of someone who represented the majority view among Irish people during the 20th century. His life was rooted in the community in which he lived; his time in the Dáil was to work on their behalf, not to lobby for himself to obtain a position in the government.

One evening he was to attend a dinner of the local Fianna Fail party in a local town. He invited me to accompany him, on one condition – not speak a word and reveal the suspect Brit accent.

It was an unforgettable evening. It was the height of the Troubles; emotions were running high among both communities. The dinner began in a sober way, with soup and the main course, and speeches on the achievements of the Fianna Fail government. There were songs from the rich Republican repertoire. As generous servings of Guinness and whiskey took effect, tongues were loosened and the anti-British and anti-Loyalist rhetoric became more virulent. Clutching the microphone, one man proposed that everyone drive together to Belfast and attack the British army. Dr Gibbons pulled the microphone away from the man so that we could hear him no more. As the Member of Parliament and senior party member in the room, he was in a position to calm the situation. How grateful I was to take heed of his order to remain silent.

After his retirement from his medical practice, he remained

active in the community in social and economic development programmes, in Gaelic games organisations, but also finding time to perform as an actor in the local amateur drama group, and speaking the Irish language he loved when the occasion arose. He died on 14 November 2007, at the age of 91. The future Taoiseach, Brian Cowan, came to Keadue for the funeral. The Taoiseach at the time, Bertie Ahern, said in his published tribute:

> "He lived a long life to the brim of achievement and public service and was one of Roscommon's favourite sons. In community life, in politics and in his profession, Hugh Gibbons made a sizeable difference. He will be long remembered in his native county for the positive and generous role he played in its development."

My knowledge and understanding of Ireland was greatly enriched through knowing him.

Many people in the North sought relief from the pressure of the Troubles by crossing the border into the south for weekends and holidays. Keadue was one option – convenient, just over the border. In the summer of 1978, I decided to attend Writers Week in Listowel, a town of 5,000 people in County Kerry in the far southwest. I invited a friend named Trevor Hoyle, a professional author from Rochdale in the north of England. The festival began in 1970 and had become one of Ireland's most important literary events.

After we arrived in the town, we were invited to meet Mick Barry, a local dairy farmer. This visit was memorable for two reasons. Mick was a railway enthusiast and had collected pieces of the Lartigue Monorail, which ran 14.4 kilometres between Listowel and Ballybunion from 1888 to 1924. It was unlike any other railway in the world because the rails lay not on the ground but in the air balanced on each other. Designed by French engineer Charles Lartigue, it was built at waist height on A shaped-trestles. Mick delighted visitors to the farm by showing one of the last sections of the line still in existence. Then he invited us to sit in his front room overlooking a large lawn, with his cows in a field behind.

We asked him how he had been affected by membership of the European Common Market, which Ireland had joined in January 1973.

"It is like green money falling out of the sky," he said. He explained that, before membership, he would each morning call the local creamery and ask if they wanted the milk he and his wife had just drawn from his fifty cows. "Half the time, they said they did not. Since we had no way to store the milk for a long time, we poured it away. But, under the Common Agricultural Policy (CAP), the creamery buys all our milk. I do not need to call them but take the milk each morning in our pick-up truck. We have a guaranteed buyer and a guaranteed price," he said with a big smile.

We did not realise it at the time but membership of the Common Market and the CAP would transform Ireland from one of the poorest countries in Europe to one of the richest, in the space of less than fifty years. According to figures from the European Union, between 1973 and 2004, Irish farmers like Mick received 54 billion euros from the CAP. Between 1973 and 2015, Ireland received over 74.3 billion euros from the EU and contributed about 32 billion—a net gain of 42.3 billion. Unknown to us, on the lush green fields of Listowel, a silent revolution was in progress. The other thing I remember from the visit was the warmth of the welcome. Mick had never met Trevor or me, but he treated us like long-lost friends.

The next item in Listowel was the Book Festival. Here is a

letter I wrote to a friend about the event.

"On the Saturday morning three authors launched their books. Each spoke for five minutes, summarising the contents very briefly and following up with three jokes and, in one case, three comic songs. The comic vein continued at a lunch to which Trevor and I were invited by a Captain (Irish army or IRA, who knows). After the food, we got back to the mood of the book launching, with comic stories, songs and mimicry of a high order. For me, the star of thc week was John B. Keane."

Keane was the most famous author from Listowel, with a statue of him in the town square. He was a prolific author, of novels, plays and essays. He is the uncle of Fergal Keane, a well-known author and investigative journalist with the BBC. "He has sold 1.5 million paperback copies of his plays and books (out of a population of three million!)," I wrote. "His skill is his ear; he writes what people tell him and what he hears over the counter. He holds up the mirror of Irish society, warts and all, and the Irish people—you know how malicious and prudish they can be—love it ... During the week, I felt the strength and weakness of this nation—wit, imagination and a lust in discussing anything and anyone without reserve or respect. Against that, too small a circuit, too small a subject—endlessly, Unity and Partition, like bad weather over any sunshine. The welcome was warm and meant; honesty and open-ness greeted us everywhere. Trevor loved it after the circumspection he meets in England. Another ugly face was drink and alcoholism, which helped to fuel the country's tourist industry. It is result was driving fatalities, political, criminal and domestic violence, a quarter of a million Pioneers (who abstain from alcohol) and an enormous health risk. Minister of Health and Social Services Charles Haughey had a brainwave—give up both drink and fags. One wag commented, 'he is no longer Minister of Finance.'"

"Another ambiguity is the vitality, energy and good spirits we met," I continued. "Its other face is violence. A friend told me that, in a spirit of pilgrimage, Haughey goes to Tralee, County Kerry to visit Liam Mullins, one of the most senior IRA civil war and Independence men still alive. Mullins scoffs at the politicians – 'We created the state, we created the conditions in which these men operate. It is violence which won us our freedom, it is violence which will do it now.'"

Haughey was one of the most important political leaders of his generation. A member of the Irish Parliament from 1957 to 1992, he served three times as Taoiseach for a total of more than seven years. He was leader of the Fianna Fail party founded by Eamon De Valera and to which Dr Hugh Gibbons belonged.

Once I had the opportunity to interview him. It was early on a Saturday morning, at Abbeville, a historic house with 100 hectares of land, which Haughey had bought in 1969. One previous owner was John Beresford, an Anglo-Irish politician. On that cold grey morning, I boarded a bus for the ride from Dublin to Kinsealy, north of the city where the house was located. I asked my fellow travellers for their opinion of Haughey.

"He is a sharp, clever man, probably corrupt," one said. "How else could he afford such an enormous house, with stables and horses? If he can make as much money for us as he did for himself, we would all be rich." I remember little of what Haughey said; he was too clever a politician to reveal anything new to a rookie reporter like me, especially one with the wrong accent. What I remember is the imposing mansion, the long corridors and the fields stretching into the distance. The symbolism was very clear – a mansion that had belonged to the Anglo-Irish elite was now in the hands of a new ruling class.

Another memorable thing happened during our visit to County Kerry. One day a friend invited us to the beach. It was a warm, lazy afternoon and the beach was not crowded. In our swimming trunks and towels over our shoulders, we went to chat with a group of people a short distance away. Also dressed in beach attire, they were extremely friendly. After a few minutes, we realised that the man talking to us was no ordinary Paddy but Garrett Fitzgerald, who had been Foreign Minister until his Fine Gael party suffered a landslide defeat in June 1977. He became leader of the Opposition, the position he held when we met him. He talked eloquently about Ireland's position in the European Common Market and the need for a pluralist Ireland, in which the Protestants of the North felt at home. His mother came from an Ulster Protestant family. I was blown away. In what other country in Europe could you converse casually with a former Foreign Minister on a beach without being chased away by bodyguards or secretaries? From that day forth, Fitzgerald became my favourite Irish politician. He went on to have a distinguished career, serving as Taoiseach for six years in the 1980s. He was always a leading public intellectual, writing articles and giving speeches. He spoke French fluently and did so often at EU meetings in Brussels, often to the annoyance of monolingual British officials in the room. He was the face of a new, educated and liberal Ireland, a symbol of its transformation after it joined Europe. This was a country I was happy to belong to.

The easiest way to escape the Troubles was to take the train to Dublin, a journey of two hours. Belfast railway station was conveniently located in the city centre and there were trains throughout the day. Occasionally, the line was closed or services delayed by the threat of a paramilitary bomb; but that was unusual.

The contrast between the two cities was startling. In Dublin, there were no army patrols or road blocks, peace walls or poignant graffiti. It was relaxed and normal, a typical busy European capital, where people hurried on their way to the office or the department store. You could walk on banks of the River Liffey, which runs east to west through the city; you could sit peacefully in cafes and pubs outside, enjoying the 'craic' (banter). The first thing that struck those of us visiting from the North was people's lack of interest in what was happening there. Seven years into the Troubles, the people of Dublin, and of the South in general, had become numb to the constant bad news. In Belfast, we dissected each bombing and killing: who was the target and the reason for the operation? What does it tell us of the wider war? "No thanks, we do not want to hear of it," said Dublin people. "Let me get on with my life and you keep the madness to yourself." Very few Southerners went to the North, except for urgent family or business events – not to speak of people from Britain or Europe; its once flourishing tourism business was dead. I could not persuade members of my own family to come, even for a weekend. My only visitors were journalists, driven by professional curiosity.

During my three and a half years in the North, Dublin was largely spared the violence. Loyalist paramilitaries carried out three bombing attacks there; one killed an employee of Dublin Airport and injured eight civilians. Republican paramilitaries killed a suspected informer, a leader of a Republican faction and an English salesman suspected of helping the British Army. This low level of violence was due to the fact that Loyalist groups felt unsafe operating too far from their bases; they preferred easier targets in the North. For their part, Republican groups did not want to damage the South's economy. We should also credit the intelligence gathering of the South's security forces and their ability to pre-empt attacks; it was hard to know which was more important. But as a result, the Dublin we saw was normal and bustling; an economic transformation that had begun with entry into the European Common Market on January 1, 1973 continued and the island's tourism industry thrived.

Between 1965 and 2000, the number of overseas visitors increased almost five-fold and foreign exchange earnings from tourism rose forty-fold. Figures from Bord Failte (Tourism Board) show the number of overseas visitors to Ireland rose from 1.28 million in 1973 to 2.098 million in 1987, 3.348 million in 1993 and 4.231 million in 1995. Of these, tourists accounted for 1.14 million in 1973 to 1.425 million in 1987, 1.839 million in 1993 and 2.243 million in 1995. These figures show the success of the South in insulating itself from the Troubles in the North. They lasted from 1969 to the Good Friday Agreement (GFA) in April 1998. During this period, the South was able to increase nearly four-fold the number of foreign visitors.

The Troubles changed the view of Southern people. The Irish constitution of 1937 did not recognise British jurisdiction over the North and said that the whole island belonged to the new state; a large majority in the South agreed. But the violence of the Troubles, and the virulent opposition of many Protestants, made many change their minds.

"If the country were united, how would we integrate and manage these hardliners?" said Liam O'Brien, a schoolteacher. "Better have the British Army do it. We are not ready for this."

Over the next years, this became the position of the Irish government, although it could not say so in public and deny articles two and three of the constitution. In the GFA, the Irish government removed these two articles and said that it was up to the Northern Ireland people themselves to decide their own future; for unification, a majority of people on both sides of the border must vote for it. This was a very sensible outcome; history may ask why all the parties could not have signed the GFA ten or twenty years earlier and how much pain and suffering it would have saved. Irish officials told me that the best unification would be slow and gradual. If you force a lady to marry you, the union will not last. Woo her with gifts, roses and good behaviour and you may win her over. Under the GFA, the British Secretary of State is obliged to call a referendum if a majority in the North "would express a wish for a united Ireland". That is indeed a grave responsibility; he or she should think a thousand times before taking a decision. If 51 per cent voted for unity, how could the South convince the other 49 per cent and integrate them well into a new state?

In April 2018, Arlene Foster, then leader of the Democratic Unionist Party, the largest pro-British party, said that, if Ireland were united, she would probably leave. "If it were to happen, I'm not sure that I would be able to continue to live here, I would feel so strongly about it," she said.

Many Unionists may follow her example. So the process of reconciliation has only just began. My advice to the Secretary of State: do not call a referendum.

There was much to do in Dublin as well as discuss these heavy subjects. One evening a friend invited me to the Abbey Theatre to see "Conn The Shaughraun", a play by Dion Boucicault. Born in Dublin in December 1820, he was an Irish actor and playwright famous for his melodramas; he wrote and performed in them in Britain and the United States, where he died in September 1890. This is what I wrote about the performance in a letter to a friend in January 1976: "The hero of this melodrama was a poacher/skinflint/criminal who avoided prison and penury by astute use of his tongue and sharp wit in difficult circumstances. At the end, the thunderous applause of the audience permits him to marry his woman, which the priest in the play forbids. Though it was not a very good plot, I laughed myself stupid. Comic genius in rags – the story of this island."

Another bonus of going to Dublin was to attend matches of hurling and Gaelic football at Croke Park. These are organised by the Gaelic Athletic Association (GAA), which is, like the Abbey Theatre, a child of the Gaelic Revival at the end of the 19th century. The theatre opened on December 27 1904, while the GAA was founded in Hayes Hotel, Thurles, County Tipperary on November 1, 1884. From the beginning, its association with nationalist politics brought it to the attention of the British authorities. On 'Bloody Sunday', November 21, 1920, British soldiers opened fire on both players and crowds in attendance at a Gaelic football match in Croke Park; they killed Michael Hogan, a Tipperary footballer, and thirteen spectators. This was part of a sweeping-up exercise after the assassination that morning of what were believed to be fifteen secret service intelligence officers by the IRA, directed by Michael Collins. One of the stands at Croke Park is today named after Michael Hogan. Given the GAA's nationalist affiliations, members of the army or police forces under British rule were not allowed to play Gaelic games, a source of considerable tension in Northern Ireland during recent decades of conflict. The rule was only removed during the Peace Process.

In terms of membership and revenue, the GAA has been the most successful product of the Irish cultural revival. Irish writer Daniel Corkery famously described the fervour of the crowd at a hurling championship final as "the national type of Ireland." In 2019, the GAA announced record revenue of 73.9 million euros, up 16 per cent on 2018. It has a global membership of more than 500,000. Thousands of women also play Gaelic sports, both football and camogie, a variant of hurling. Most astonishingly, it remains an amateur sport. While rugby, cricket and especially soccer pay grotesque salaries to their star players, those in GAA teams receive only expenses and the glory of representing their county; players cannot be sold or transferred from one county to another. They receive their reward in local fame and popularity, which they can convert into good jobs and, sometimes, a seat in the Dail. Perhaps this is the reason why attendances for GAA games are the highest of any sport in Ireland; the spectators feel a close bond between themselves and the players as part of the same county and community. How can a Brazilian or Ukrainian playing for a soccer team in Turin, Paris or Manchester feel such a connection?

Croke Park has a capacity of 82,300 spectators, making it the third largest stadium in Europe. The games I attended, writing stories for the UK press, were All-Ireland finals, when the stadium was full. They were boisterous and passionate events, but without the violence that sometimes scars major football games in European cities. We marveled at the skill of the players, especially in hurling in which you must control with a hand or flat stick a small ball, the sliotar, travelling through the air at high speed. My sense was that the spectators were especially proud at these finals, not only to see their county play but also because this was the national game, a symbol of the independent state. Gaelic sports bind the people of Ireland together. These finals rank among the most important days of the year; Irish people fly home from abroad to attend them. The GAA spends its substantial revenues on improving the large stadia as well as facilities at the local level. This means that fans can see where their money is going, into projects from which they and their children will benefit.

The length of Croke Park is three soccer fields, with its width one soccer field. The players of Gaelic sports, at home and abroad, are nearly all Irish. However, in Hong Kong, I attended an Asian Gaelic sports tournament and was astonished to see

Chinese, Koreans and Japanese play.

Once I was chatting to a middle-aged lady next to a park in west Belfast. "How many children do you have?" I asked.

"By the grace of God, eight," she replied with a big smile. "Two of them have gone into the priesthood. What a blessing for the whole family. It means that, whatever sins we commit, all the family will be able to go straight to heaven."

In the South of Ireland, as in Republican areas of the North, the power and authority of the Roman Catholic church were everywhere. Their imposing buildings—churches, schools, hospitals, seminaries and parish houses—towered over the modest streets around them. Where priests walked, people smiled and bowed before them. For a Catholic family, to have a son or daughter in the church was a blessing and an honour. During my years there, Ireland had about 3,900 priests; a sharp decline did not begin until 1990. In accordance with the teachings of the church, the state banned contraception, abortion and divorce. This was hard to believe in a modern European state. Everyone knew that the rich and well-connected could obtain condoms and contraceptives and arrange abortions abroad; it was the poor, less educated and less informed who paid the heaviest price. It was they who were left with children they did not want and the social disgrace it could bring. Some women had to leave their hometown or village, or even leave Ireland all together. At his public hospital in London in the 1960s, my father had many patients, young and unmarried, who had come from Ireland to seek an abortion. Under British law, the procedure required the assent of two doctors; many did not want to accept such patients, but my father was willing.

In April 1968, the Abortion Act 1967, passed by the British Parliament six months before, came into effect. It made abortion legal on a wide number of grounds up to 28 weeks' gestation throughout Great Britain, but not Northern Ireland. The women who asked for my father's help were alone and frightened; they dared not tell their families and friends at home. It was a long journey by boat across the Irish Sea and then train to London. They were counting the days of their pregnancy and did not know what they would find on arrival. It was a fearful ordeal for a young lady in a strange land. How many more did not have the money or means to make the journey?

One relative in London employed as a maid Kathleen, a woman from a village in the South of Ireland. When she became pregnant with a child outside marriage, the parish priest banished her. The baby was given to her mother to bring up as her own, the "youngest child" in the family—a common occurrence. Kathleen was traumatised and developed epilepsy as a result; when prospective employers in England found out, they refused to hire her. Fortunately, my relative was generous and took her on. Sometimes, because of her illness, she dropped to the ground; fortunately, she was only carrying dishes or clothes, not a baby. She was given limited access to her child at home; she was introduced to the child as her "elder sister". With medication, she was able to control the epilepsy and found it easier to get work. In her thirties, she married a Jewish barber in London; they had a child of their own. The cruelty of that parish priest and the pervasive culture ruined her life; was this the Christian spirit?

With the co-operation of the state, the Church established mother and baby homes called Magdalen Laundries, where unmarried pregnant women were sent to have their babies. Some never escaped from these institutions. Most of the babies died or were adopted; they were often sent overseas to couples seeking children. The mothers worked in the laundries, which brought revenue to the Religious Orders. Revelations from the late 20th century showed that many of the women suffered cruel and inhuman treatment in the laundries. They were a terrible stain on the reputation of the Church. But we only learnt later about this.

In September 1979, John Paul II went to Ireland, the first such visit by a Pope. An estimated 2.7 million people attended events during the three-day visit, more than half the population of the island. After his native Poland, was there a more Catholic nation on earth? Things changed dramatically later, but that is how it was during my time in Ireland. The church's hold over the political leaders and their reluctance to challenge it was remarkable. In 1929, the government set up the Censorship of Publications Board, to examine books and periodicals. It used criteria similar to those of the church; it banned books it considered "obscene" and "indecent"; these included many of the most famous Irish books of the next fifty years. The Film Censorship Board was set up in 1923. Over the next 60 years, it banned 2,500 films and cut 11,000. Among those banned were Scarface (1932), Clockwork Orange (1971) and Monty Python's Life of Brian (1979). The effect of this censorship was limited by the fact that people in the Republic could watch television from Northern Ireland and Britain; every month thousands crossed the Irish Sea and bought material banned at home. "There was no sex in Ireland before television," was a common saying.

What struck me was the disconnect between the strict censorship and the habits and thinking of those whom it was intended to protect. The church was authoritarian and top-down in its governance. It ran most of the country's schools and believed Protestants should be converted; they were often called 'pagans' – Protestantism was an error that needed to be corrected. John Charles McQuaid was Archbishop of Dublin and Catholic Primate of Ireland from 1940 and 1972. During this period, he was one of the most powerful men in the country, exercising great influence over social policy; he was a close friend of Eamon DeValera and one of the architects of the 1937 Constitution. In an interview with the BBC in 2019, Fintan O'Toole, a journalist with *The Irish Times*, described a visit in the 1960s by Archbishop McQuaid to his church after the death of the parish priest. "He arrived in a Bentley with a chauffeur in uniform. I saw two little feet appearing out of the car and the chauffeur kneeling on the pavement to clean them. It was the same ambience as the British Queen was visiting a town in England." In 1944, Archbishop McQuaid wrote to the government asking that it ban the sales of Tampax sanitary tampons for women.

I met many priests. Some like Father Desmond Wilson were close to their parishioners and worked hard for them; they won my admiration. During the Troubles, people desperately needed the care and support of their priests. Others were more like bureaucrats; they enjoyed the moral authority, social status and material comforts of the island's most powerful institution. They rigorously enforced the directives of the church, however much they were at variance with the needs of their parishioners. The greatest tension was over sex and marriage. In the confession box, priests heard women speak of their distress, torn between fear of pregnancy and fear of hell if they disobeyed the church. Many were in marriages in which they could not refuse the demands of their husbands. In other countries of Europe, priests found a way to square the circle – in public follow the doctrine, but in private approve contraception – but not in Ireland. Then there were stories of abuses by priests. In the pub, a person told you, after a few drinks, that his local priest had a live-in housekeeper who was his common-life wife and some had children. Occasionally, some spoke of a priest's sexual abuses with young men. But none of this appeared in the media or the public space; criticism of the church and priests was taboo. If someone had suffered abuse, he or she did not dare to say it in public; the shame was unbearable, they would not be believed and pressure from the family overwhelming. Everyone knew that the church would support the word of a priest against that of an accuser and society would support it. The Protestants in Northern Ireland recognised well this clerical dominance of government and society in the South; it convinced them they were right to create a separate state in 1922 and live under British law. Any discussion of a united island would first have to address and resolve this issue of the coalition of Church and State relationships. After Vatican 2, interchurch relations improved and the Good Friday Agreement of 1998 resolved some of the issues

Unknown to the public at that time, terrible scandals were unfolding within the church. In the early 1970s, the Bishop of Kerry Eamonn Casey had a sexual relationship with an American woman, Annie Murphy. Their son Peter was born in Dublin in 1974. Casey was determined that the child be given away for adoption; but his mother refused and took him back to the United States. Casey gave money toward Peter's maintenance but refused to develop a relationship with him. Disappointed by this, Murphy contacted *The Irish Times*; it printed the story in the early 1990s. Bishop Casey made a public apology, resigned as bishop and left the country. Then other women made allegations of sexual abuse against him. From the 1990s onwards, more scandals of this kind and of pedophilia came out, some stretching back decades. It became clear that the church had covered up the abuses. When they became public, they seriously affected vocations, attendance at Mass and the moral authority of the Church among the public. In 1998, only 44 priests were ordained in Ireland, down from a peak of 412 in 1965. In 1998, 172 priests died and 38 left the ministry – a net loss of 166 in the year. Today the church is facing a crisis. It can no longer care for parishes in the way it once could.

But all this was for the future. During the 1970s, attendance at Mass attendance remained popular, an average of more than eighty percent of believers in Ireland, and the prestige of the church high. It played a vital role in society, as a moral compass and help to individuals. It bound communities together, ran schools, universities, welfare institutions, sports clubs and charities to help the needy at home and abroad, and acted as a social unit for the believers. The church was closely associated with the Gaelic Athletic Association (GAA), which was organised at the parish level. The Church trained thousands of Irish men and women to serve as priests and nuns in Africa, Asia and elsewhere in the world. It gave them opportunities in a country with few jobs at home and where many had no alternative to emigration. Many missionaries served their new communities with love and distinction; they were among the best ambassadors of Ireland to the world. I would meet many of them later in Hong Kong. Most of what I saw was positive. The lives of the faithful were enriched by their membership. The darker side of which we learnt in later years was hidden from sight.

Nowhere was this faith more evident than the annual pilgrimage on the last Sunday in July each year to Croagh Patrick (St Patrick's Stack). This is a mountain 764 metres high, eight kilometres from Westport, County Mayo. In July 1976, I joined about 20,000 pilgrims in climbing the mountain. Many were barefoot, as an act of penance. Tradition has it that St Patrick, the patron saint of Ireland who brought Christianity to the island, fasted and prayed on the summit of the mountain in 441 AD. There is a small chapel there, Masses are celebrated and confessions heard. Each year the mountain attracts about one million pilgrims. On the last Sunday in July, over 25,000 pilgrims came to climb. According to its Visitors Centre, "the tradition of pilgrimage to this holy mountain stretches back over 5,000 years from the Stone Age to the present day without interruption. Its religious significance dates back to the time of the pagans, when people are thought to have gathered here to celebrate the beginning of harvest season."

My visit was an opportunity to talk to the pilgrims. I was impressed by their faith and eagerness to use the day as a day of penance and self-reflection. It was a pure form of piety, far from the controversies over doctrine and rumours of bad behaviour by priests. At the base of the mountain were hotels and centres for pilgrims; among them were the sick and handicapped who had come to seek divine help for their affliction. It was inspiring to see the hope and faith in their eyes. It was the Irish equivalent of Lourdes in France and Fatima in Portugal. A priest I met kindly invited me to a lunch with his colleagues. For the church, Croagh Patrick was an important place. Around the table there were a dozen men of the cloth, including the parish priest. Women brought the dishes and served us. In my life, I had never been together with so many priests. After the opening prayers, the conversation became light-hearted and comical, with jokes aimed at the parish priest, which he gently rebutted. The subtext was the great power which he wielded over everyone in the room. He could banish them from his parish and send a damaging report on them to the church hierarchy; the jokes were an ironic compliment to this power. This was the masculine world in which the priests lived; it had its own rules, topics and taboos. Fortunately, there were not too many jokes about the ignoramus who had stumbled in their midst.

Sister Mary Aquinas, who cured Hong Kong of tuberculosis.

9

The Irish Nun who beat Tuberculosis in Hong Kong

The next stop on the journey was Hong Kong, where I moved in November 1978, to work for Radio Hong Kong, the government station. To my great surprise, I found 3,000 Irish people there working in many fields, including judges, lawyers, policemen, doctors, teachers and priests, one of whom was a member of the Legislative Council. I had not expected to meet so many Irish men and women.

This Irish presence was not immediately evident. There was no consulate and few Irish brands, other than Guinness, Bailey's and other spirits. As time passed, however, I found many Irish people living and working here, in the government and the private sector. Irish independence had made no difference; British colonial governments around the world continued to recruit Irish people and work for them, as they had since the start of the empire. Irish people had better salaries and opportunities and lower taxes than at home, as I had. Only the most senior posts were closed to them – that required a British passport.

In June 1979, I wrote two articles for *The Irish Times* on the community here. It was an eye-opener, to discover the breadth and depth of their contribution. "3,000 Irish people live in Hong Kong. Many work for the Hong Kong government as policemen, architects, engineers and lawyers. Four of the 13 High Court judges are Irish; the chief of police, Brian Slevin, was born in Dartry and served in the Irish Army before joining the British police in Palestine and coming here in 1949. The head of the Special Branch is Irish, as well as the professor of engineering at Hong Kong University and the man who founded credit unions in the colony. For many of them, high salaries and a tax rate of 15 per cent were the attraction." Among the most remarkable was Sister Mary Aquinas, a Columban Sister from Ballinasloe, County Galway. After training as a doctor in Ireland, she was one of twelve Columban nuns on their way to China in 1949. But the new Communist government expelled foreign missionaries and she came to Hong Kong. She went to work at the Ruttonjee Sanatorium, established in 1949 to fight tuberculosis.

'As fate would have it, this institute opened two weeks before we arrived,' she said. 'It is named after a Parsee whose daughter died of TB and who gave the money to convert it to a TB hospital. It needed staff and here were 12 nuns with nowhere to go.'

In 1949, the death rate from tuberculosis in Hong Kong was 208 a year per 100,000. In 1979, it had fallen to 10 per 100,000. It was a remarkable success story.

'We have to thank drugs mostly,' Sister Aquinas said. 'Inoculation of babies began in 1952, and the Chinese will take anything for their health.' With the reduction in TB cases, the institute took chest and lung patients of all kinds. 'We never have a spare bed. There are 7,000 outpatients at any time. Compared to rural Asia, the public health system in HK is excellent – cheap and accessible. Long waiting lists, yes, but emergency treatment is first class.'

Probably the best known Irishman in Hong Kong at the time was another religious figure, the Rev Patrick McGovern, who had been since 1976 a member of the Legislative Council, one of the two bodies that advised the Governor on policy ... He was picked because he was a critic of government, on social and labour issues. A Jesuit, he too was trained for China but came to Hong Kong in 1955 as a teacher. Ten years later, he ran a social centre for Caritas, the welfare organisation, and his involvement with the poor began. The Communist-led riots of 1967 inspired him to found the Industrial Relations Institute, to provide workers with education on their rights and the law and with help how to organise. It wanted to offer non-political trade unions. Since then, 10,000 people had gone through the institute's courses and Father McGovern had become an advisor in many labour disputes.

He sat on five committees, including public accounts and police complaints, so he was right in the thick of it. He was especially proud of a Bill that raised the number of compulsory days off during the year, including Sundays, from 54 to 69. The Governor told him that it was he alone who piloted the Bill through unchanged.

'I accept the present system, undemocratic as it is," I quoted him as saying. 'Living standards for all have gone up in the last 10 years, no doubt about that. I want better sick leave, paid holidays, medical benefits, spread the wealth more equitably.'

In 1978, he received an honorary OBE. 'For me, the satisfaction of 27 years in HK has been to see the colony absorb millions of refugees – last year we took in 100,000 – and without help from anyone give them a good quality of life, in jobs, housing medical and legal help.'

Desmond O'Reilly Mayne, barrister and graduate of Trinity, was the Director of Legal Aid. His staff of 200 dealt with two-thirds of civil cases and 99 per cent of criminal cases in Hong Kong. His career since coming here in 1952 had included magistrate, crown counsel, director of public prosecutions and private practice to which he intends to return next year. Born in Uganda of an engineer planter who also served the British Crown, he also worked in private practice in Ireland. 'The tax laws, lack of incentive and nepotism drove me out here.'

When he arrived, the population on Hong Kong was two million and the tallest building ten storeys. By the time I spoke to him, they were building up to 50, and the view from his office was a forest of skyscrapers matched only in a few American cities. 'I can see the results of our work. Look at the boom. And the rule of law has prevailed throughout.'

Even against corruption, I asked?

'Yes, the problem of corruption, especially in the police, was much worse than we knew. But, with the Independent Commission against Corruption, it'd be a brave, I should say, a foolish man who would accept anything now.'"

Many Irish jockeys made their mark in Hong Kong, include Johnny Roe, nine times champion jockey of Ireland. Forfive years, Roe had been coming to Hong Kong for most of the racing season, which extends from October to May.

'As a jockey in Hong Kong, I am like a film star," he said. "Interest here is fantastic. I cannot walk a hundred yards down the street without being recognised. There is so much coverage on television and in the papers. On average, I have two meetings a week, with six to 10 rides. The standard is improving all the time, though it is still well behind Ireland. It is very competitive. If you do not win often enough, your licence for next season will not be renewed.'

The owner of one horse whom Roe rode to victory gave him a gold-plated putter, a new set of graphite gold clubs, a holiday in Taiwan and flew his wife and three children out to Hong Kong.

Yet another was Tim McNeill, director of Guinness (HK) and secretary of the St Patrick's Society, which boasted 260 members, two monthly social functions and charity work. The Guinness in Hong Kong had to be imported via a bottling plant in Liverpool.

'We sell 4.5 million bottles a year. In Hong Kong, 80 per cent of the beer is drunk at home, so the secret is to get it into the groceries and supermarkets.' He said he was helped by a belief in some quarters that Guinness is an aphrodisiac, and babies should be washed in it, to give them vitality.

The St Patrick's Society was founded in 1931. Its first president was a Joseph Horsford Kemp, who arrived in Hong Kong in 1898. A Cantonese speaker, he had a distinguished career in the judiciary; he was Attorney General from 1915 to 1930 and Chief Justice from 1930 to 1933. The society was the long-running institution of Irish people in the colony. The highlight of its social calendar was the St Patrick's Ball, held in one of the city's top hotels; the attendants dined and danced to an Irish music group invited for the occasion. After arrival in Hong Kong, I joined and paid HK$300 for two tickets to the ball on March 17, 1979.

Another person I interviewed for the article was Christelle Molloy, from Holy Cross, County Tipperary. She arrived in Hong Kong in November 1976 and sold Spanish lollipops and Chupa Chups, for which her husband had the exclusive Southeast Asia franchise.

"My advice to anyone – don't come without a job and a skill," she said. "Hong Kong is a great place for business. Everyone works hard and there's none of that dreadful moaning and lethargy you get in Europe."

How perceptive she was, I thought. Going to work abroad was not only about salary, tax rates and opportunities for promotion; it was also a form of personal liberation, leaving behind the prying eyes and the chattering tongues of your home town. Here you had no history; you could start with a clean slate. That was attractive for the Irish emigrants, as it was for other foreigners. I found that most Irish people lived in the expatriate, rather than the Chinese, world. Outside work, foreigners had schools, bars and restaurants, and social, sports and recreation clubs and associations that catered to them.

Father McGovern was one of dozens of Irish priests and nuns in Hong Kong. I discovered that, between 1926 and 1970, 106 Irish Jesuits had come to the city. They ran two of Hong Kong's best secondary schools: served the homeless, the poor and the handicapped: worked as chaplains to the police and seamen. One reforested the city after World War Two and headed the Department of Agriculture. They set up civic organisations which have thrived long after the priests ceased to manage them. They lived in a different way to most foreigners. They learnt Cantonese and have lived and worked with Chinese people, not expatriates. They devoted their adult lives to the people of Hong Kong. Most did not retire to Ireland, and are buried in St Michael's Catholic Cemetery in Happy Valley.

There were priests and nuns from other orders, including the Columbans, the Salesians and the La Salle Brothers, as well as ministers from the Church of Ireland. They worked in schools and universities, in hospitals, churches and in social welfare. Their contribution to the education, health and pastoral care of the people of Hong Kong has been immeasurable. These religious people, like my Grandfather in Manchuria, were like other foreigners in Hong Kong in that working abroad gave them opportunities and relationships they could never have at home. They exchanged the village and small town of their childhood for a teeming housing estate in Hong Kong; its tenants were eager to attend their schools, hospitals and social centres. It was a great challenge to adapt to a new culture and a new language; it was also a liberation and an inspiration. Before Ireland joined the European Communities (now the European

Union) on January 1 1973, it was one of the poorest countries in western Europe, heavily reliant on agriculture and with a high level of emigration. Missionary service overseas was one of the most rewarding careers, to both men and women.

In June 1980, I interviewed Taoiseach Jack Lynch on his way home after a ten-day visit to China. Lynch had resigned as Taoiseach in December 1979 but remained a T.D. He had ninety minutes of talks with Deng Xiaoping, the most powerful man in China. Here is part of my report which *The Irish Times* published on June 12, 1980:

> "Mr and Mrs Lynch saw the new embassy in Peking. It is large enough to provide accommodation for all the staff there, thereby solving the biggest headache facing most foreigners in Peking. When the previous occupants left, they took the toilets with them – leaving just 'Shanghai closets', as holes in the floor are discreetly known. However, carpets are being flown out from Ireland and staff from the Office of Public Works are there to assist with advice and purchasing."

This move into the former Iraqi embassy proved to be an excellent and foresightful move. The government in Beijing designated the areas for foreign embassies; the space was limited. The new embassy was spacious and centrally located; the ambassador and his staff did well to persuade the Foreign Ministry to allocate the site to them.

My own modest place in the Hong Kong universe was as a news reader and reporter in the English news section of the government Radio Television Hong Kong (RTHK). I was greatly helped by one of my superiors at BBC Radio Ulster; he had worked at RTHK for eight years and kindly wrote a letter of recommendation.

After 140 years, the Hong Kong government had long experience of breaking in new arrivals like me. My colleagues at RTHK were extremely helpful in explaining how everything worked. I was allocated a small apartment in a block for expatriate civil servants close to the Central business district where we had our office. The rent was one sixth of an apartment of the same size in the commercial market; I paid HK$200 a month to a lady to clean the apartment and my clothes. The block was guarded by two dogs and frequent police visits. The commute was a pleasant walk down a steep hillside, through an area full of trees, streams and tropical plants and past some colonial buildings used as homes and offices for government staff. What a blessing compared to the exhausting road and rail commutes of people in most cities around the world.

Gradually, the colonial system under which the British ruled Hong Kong—and of which I was a beneficiary—became clear. The majority of staff in government departments were Hong Kong Chinese, with a limited number of expatriates holding middle and the most senior positions. In RTHK, all the staff in the Cantonese news section were Chinese; in the English section, there were British, Irish, Australians, Indians, Chinese and one man from Rhodesia, later Zimbabwe. He had been in the military, so when independence approached, he had to leave. The top positions in RTHK were held, as in other departments, by expatriates, mainly British.

There was an embarrassing gap in knowledge between expats and our Chinese colleagues. They read the Chinese newspapers, watched Chinese television and knew so much more about Hong Kong and China than we did. But we enjoyed better salaries and conditions, and free medical and dental care; after fulfilling a contract of two and a half years, we received a paid holiday of three months and a gratuity of equivalent to 25 per cent of all we had earned. This was the white man's privilege. I asked one of my Chinese colleagues how he could tolerate such inequalities.

"That is the colonial system," he said. "For us, the salary and status of working in RTHK are better than other jobs and Hong Kong is infinitely better than mainland China. Since English is an official language here, RTHK must have an English service. So it must offer salaries and conditions good enough to attract gweilos (foreign devils) to work here."

As my knowledge of Cantonese improved, I discovered one way my Chinese colleagues handled this inequality – laughing at us. They had comic nicknames – often animals – to describe us. The jokes did not bring promotion or higher salaries, but at least made them feel better.

Socially, it was a time of transition from the segregation of the past. In the 1950s and 1960s, the British government and its major companies discouraged – and sometimes banned – their white male employees from marrying Chinese or other Asians. They wanted white spouses, preferably British or from a non-Communist country. The colonial government believed that a Chinese wife could be vulnerable to pressure from criminal gangs or, worse, the government in Beijing; this could force her husband to reveal information or take decisions he should not. The Foreign Office and multinational companies wanted couples whom they could transfer around the world and would mix easily with expatriate society in other countries. A British friend at one of Hong Kong's big banks fell in love with a Chinese lady in his branch.

"Fine, you can marry her if you wish," his boss told him. "But, if you do, you will become a local employee and always work in Hong Kong. You will no longer be an international officer who can be transferred to other countries in Asia."

He chose his sweetheart over his ambition and, who knows, maybe the couple lived happily ever after. By the late 1970s, such barriers were coming down. As Japan, Taiwan, Singapore, South Korea, Hong Kong and later China became wealthy, so a wife from one of these countries became an asset for a rising executive; she could help him expand his social network and win contracts.

Parties I attended often had people of all races, from different countries of Asia, as well as Chinese and expatriates. Couples were more likely to be white male and Asian female than the other way around. Inter-racial marriages were increasingly common, but they were not a simple matter. The parents of one or both parties were often suspicious, if not opposed. Did the two sets of parents share a common language? How much did each party know of the family and background of the other? In which culture would they bring up their children, the Western or the Chinese? As I learnt later, many ladies in Taiwan, China and other countries in Asia were desperate to leave their homeland; marriage with a foreigner was the quickest way out. This was less common in wealthier Hong Kong. Its people could travel, study and work abroad; many came from families able to pay for this, and the city's currency was convertible. So a foreigner was not the only exit strategy.

I played in a soccer team; our captain was John, a burly Irish police inspector from Birmingham. At a party he gave at his apartment, I met his wife – a tall, slender Chinese from Shanghai. We were wondering how the inspector had landed such a beauty. As the evening wore on, we found out. Her father was an official of the Chinese central bank in Shanghai; in December 1948, he was ordered to move the nation's gold reserves, about 115 tons, to Taiwan. Over the next months, the operation was conducted in total secrecy, by military vessels and airplanes. Completely loyal, the father carried out his duties to the letter. So, when he and his family arrived in Hong Kong, they were penniless. John commented: "If he had done what I would have done, he would have absconded to the U.S. with the loot—and I would not have met my wife!"

One Chinese colleague went to Britain for a three-month training programme. After his return, I asked how he enjoyed the visit.

"It was very surprising," he said. "I saw poor whites, badly dressed and with dirty hair. Some were alcoholics or drug addicts and lived in the streets. I never expected to see such people."

His answer made me think of the colonial 'myth'—how can a small number of people of one race rule another so much more numerous? This sense of superiority expressed by my colleague was one reason. In Hong Kong, he did not see such people; whites were well dressed, had pleasant offices and lived in comfortable apartments. He lived in a public housing estate, densely crowded; no whites lived there.

Language, of course, was a major way to enforce this superiority. When I arrived, English was still the dominant language of the government, the civil service, the police, the justice system, banks, foreign companies, the more prestigious schools and Hong Kong University. This gave an enormous advantage to those who spoke it. A Chinese who wanted a career outside the Chinese business community and his own society had to learn it.

As a reporter, I had more opportunities than many expats to have a closer look at the Chinese world in the city; priests and many policemen knew it much better than I. The best opportunity came on a Thursday evening, when I visited a colleague in the public housing estate when he lived; we chatted in Cantonese for one hour and then one hour in English. The apartment blocks in the estate had 30 storeys, with about a dozen units on each floor, ranging in size from 30-70 square metres depending on the size of the family. My colleague, Mr Wong, lived with his parents and two siblings in a unit of 60 square metres. It was crowded; the family kept it neat and tidy. Their budget was tight; both the parents had jobs that paid a low salary and demanded long hours. Mr Wong's position and prospects represented the family's best chance for advancement.

He talked about the harsh life of rationing and party study sessions they had endured in mainland China; they had moved to Hong Kong seven years before. They were delighted to enjoy the freedoms and opportunities of Hong Kong. The apartment blocks were densely populated but clean, well-lit and well-aired. There were guards at the entrance. The only Big-Nose coming in and out, I felt safe—certainly safer than entering the apartment blocks of the Easterhouses estate in Glasgow, where groups of young men were waiting to relieve you of your watch, your wallet and your dignity.

In 1978, Chinese accepted colonial rule relatively easily because of conditions in the mainland. Only two years before, the Cultural Revolution had ended with the death of Mao Tse-tung. It had been a period of economic and social chaos, with millions of city residents sent to work in the countryside; many died or fell sick there. The economy came close to collapse. For Chinese in Hong Kong, life under British rule was immeasurably better than cleaning toilets and tending pigs in a remote mountain village in the mainland. That was the alternative—not the independence dreamt of by people in Ireland and other colonies. Hong Kong had good law and order. It provided free education and subsidised housing and medical care; this was more than many countries in Asia. Ireland was Britain's first colony; it had made all its mistakes there. It had learnt from them—and Hong

Kong became one of its most successful colonies.

I was fortunate to arrive in November 1978. Just a few weeks later, the Chinese Communist Party held its Third Plenum in Beijing, at which Deng Xiaoping announced the "open-door and reform" policy. After thirty years of self-imposed isolation, China was ready to do business with the world – and Hong Kong was the city in the world best placed to benefit. Here is part of a letter to a friend dated December 13, 1980:

"I must admit to being in a sustained period of Chinese worship. Living here, I feel a member of an inferior race which by accident of history and superior military weapons has acquired a certain power that is slowly slipping away. We Europeans are living off that capital. But it will not last for much longer. By contrast, the industriousness of the Japanese, Koreans and Chinese has to be seen to be believed. Hong Kong is a place with no resources at all apart from a deep water harbour. Yet it has managed a growth rate of 10 per cent for the last 10 years and is now booming. With the opening of China, that means a double fillip. So I feel very lucky to be here. How relieved I am not to have to cover strikes, sit-ins, factory closures and demonstrations as I would have to in Britain ... Socially, this is a fine place. Manners and behaviour I find pleasantly old fashioned; girls are shy and people do not argue with you (though they disagree inside, of course). In imitation of my Chinese betters, I gave up alcohol about 15 months ago. That changes social patterns drastically, I have found. The whites think it very odd."

Everyone in Hong Kong did well out of this sudden opening up of the mainland. The city's banks, accountants, lawyers, insurers, consultants and other specialists had knowledge and experience not available to their counterparts in the mainland. Chinese firms that wanted to engage with the outside world, to import and export, and attract inward investment had to use these companies. Like other foreigners, Irish people in Hong Kong benefitted greatly from the new policy; they would continue to do so for the next thirty years.

When Christmas 1978 approached, I had been in Hong Kong less than two months and had nowhere to go. A colleague at RTHK kindly invited me to her apartment to celebrate Christmas Day. I found there her partner and a handsome young Chinese named Mr Leung. When we opened our presents, Leung unwrapped a small box – it contained an elegant porcelain penis. Everyone laughed loudly; I struggled to understand the meaning of it. Leung explained that he had a double life. To please his family, he had a girlfriend they approved of. But he was really a homosexual with a boyfriend – the one who had provided this eye-catching gift. "I have to hide this from my parents. They must have no inkling that I am gay," he said.

This opened the window for me on the gay world of Hong Kong. While Britain had decriminalised homosexuality in 1967, it had not done so in Hong Kong. So, when I arrived, it was illegal. In private, senior British officials supported a change in the law but did not implement one – Chinese society was conservative and strongly opposed any revision. Many parents saw homosexuality as a "Western disease" from which they had to protect their children. So Leung and other Chinese gays had to go to great lengths to hide their sexuality from their families and employers. Among the expats, the situation was similar to that in Britain in the years before it was legalised. Some, including those in the civil service, were gay in private; they arranged gay parties with like-minded people. But it had to be kept out of the public eye and of the media. The government was nervous that criminal gangs and agents of China or the Soviet Union would find evidence of homosexual activity of a senior official and use it to blackmail him.

In January 1980, this became headline news when the body of a young Scottish police officer, John MacLennan, was found in his locked police quarters along with a suicide note. He had apparently shot himself five times, a fact which raised eyebrows. He had been about to be charged with homosexual acts. Many did not accept the official version of suicide and suspected that he had been murdered. They believed that he was being victimised because he knew the names of gay police officers far senior to him. This caused a public outcry; the government was forced to appoint a Commission of Inquiry, which sat for eight months, at a cost of HK$16 million, a record in Hong Kong for such an inquiry.

The civil service issued an order to find the gays in its ranks; this order came to touch me. To improve my Cantonese, I had taken as a room-mate a young Chinese civil servant named Stanley. He got free boarding in a good location in exchange for talking to me in Cantonese. In the event, he worked long hours and did not have the patience or interest to teach me; he did not like me very much. Also he spent the weekends with his family in Yuen Long, at the other end of Hong Kong. But he was polite and easy to live with; it was a small way to share the white man's privilege. He was a typical example of the Hong Kong success story. In 1948, his father had escaped the Communists and settled in Hong Kong; he worked in a grocery shop in Yuen Long. Stanley studied very hard—no booze, cigarettes, drugs or other vices. He learnt English and passed the exam for Hong Kong University. How proud his father was to see his son arrive each weekend in stylish cream trousers and carrying books on Economics and Urban Planning In the Western World. Many young people made this leap from poverty to sophistication and a well-paid job in one generation.

One day I received an order to visit the Government

Secretariat and the office of a senior Chinese official, named Mr Huang. A man in his fifties, he sat behind a desk in his large office, full of books and official documents. I stood in front of the desk, nervous and out of place.

"Mr O'Neill, it has come to our attention that you share your apartment with a young Chinese man. Is that correct?" he said in flawless English.

"Yes, that is true."

"Why is he living there?"

"I wish to improve my Cantonese. I give him free lodging in exchange for his talking to me in Cantonese."

Mr Wong paused. Evidently, he did not believe this answer. Few expats learnt Cantonese. If they did, they went to lessons or bars or learnt it from films and pop songs. Invite a Chinese stranger to live in their home? No, not plausible. I waited for the next question, which should have been "Are you sleeping with him?" But Mr Wong could not ask it. A middle-aged Chinese and experienced civil servant, he probably detested homosexuality. But he felt uncomfortable putting the question to a Big-Nose. Decades of working for expats had made him deferential, even to one so much junior to him in rank. In any case, he had done the interview and could tick me off the list.

"If you have no more questions, can I go now?"

"Yes."

But the McLennan inquiry did spark a debate on the issue and in 1991, the government decriminalised private, adult, non-commercial and consensual homosexual relations.

My Grandfather with student graduates from his school in Faku.

10

The Irish and the Church in China

The greatest contribution of the Irish to China was their missionaries, both Catholic and Protestant. They built schools, hospitals, churches, orphanages, old people's homes and welfare centres. Grandfather and his fellow Presbyterians were among them.

My time in Belfast had provided a limited understanding of Grandfather's life in China—forty-five years in Faku, a small town in Liaoning province in the Northeast of China, or Manchuria as it was called in his time. Hong Kong was much closer to Faku than Belfast; so my interest in his life increased accordingly. China's open-door policy also opened the possibility of foreigners being allowed to go there.

Faku is deep in the countryside of Liaoning, ninety kilometres north of the provincial capital, Shenyang. Since 1949, like most rural areas of China, it had been closed to foreigners. Dr Jack Weir, whom we met in Chapter Three, kindly introduced me to others who had worked with Grandfather in Faku. They sent me letters that provided much valuable information about the town, the church, the life of Grandfather and the other Irish there and how they were regarded by local residents. So, in Hong Kong, I felt closer to him and better able to understand what persuaded him to go to Manchuria and sustained him while he was there.

This is what I wrote about Grandfather in a letter from Hong

Kong on January 18, 1980:

> "To go to Manchuria was like a voyage to the Moon, in terms of climate, culture, language, remoteness and an uncertain reception. What was in the hearts of those in Belfast that could convince them to give up the rest of their life to a country they had never seen and a people they had never met? How did they view the loneliness, the sexual abstinence, the discomfort of temperature and lack of goods and the services to which they were accustomed? Whatever view you take of the missionary effort, these were remarkable people."

Grandfather belonged to the Presbyterian Church of Ireland. Between 1869 and 1951, it sent 91 missionaries to Manchuria, men and women, including doctors and ministers. They established nine main mission stations, of which Faku was one, each with 20-30 outstations. Every station had a church, hospital and schools. They were part of a great multinational effort to evangelise China. The first Irishman to have made a recorded visit to China was a Franciscan friar named James. He accompanied an Italian Franciscan, Odoric of Pordenone on an extraordinary journey around the world between 1318 and 1330, fifty years after the more famous travels of Marco Polo. James joined Odoric at Ormus in India; from there, they went by sea to Sumatra and Borneo and then Guangzhou in southern China. The two men spent 1323 to 1328 travelling and preaching all over China. This included three years in Beijing at the court of the Great Khan. So there was an Irishman in the Imperial capital of China seven centuries ago!

The Presbyterians were among thousands of missionaries,

Catholic and Protestant, who served in China between 1858 and 1949, when the People's Republic was founded; the new government expelled the foreign missionaries. The earliest missionaries learnt Chinese but did not have the money or means to leave the colonial outposts of Hong Kong and Macao to spread the gospel inland. So they accepted employment on vessels of opium traders which went to Chinese ports. During the day, they worked as interpreters for foreigners negotiating with Chinese buyers. In the evenings, they went to evangelise among the local population. Such work was illegal; a Chinese found to be involved could receive a death sentence. Then, in 1860, the government was forced to change its policy as part of the humiliating terms of the Convention of Beijing, following its defeat in the Second Opium War. The convention both legalised the opium trade and gave foreigners the right to spread Christianity. So Chinese were correct to point out that evangelisation had only become possible because of a war fought to legalise the import of opium; it was an extremely lucrative business for foreign companies, especially British ones which imported shipments from India. "Opium in one hand and a Bible in the other", was an accusation which many Chinese have made, right up to the present day. Many missionaries felt uncomfortable with this immoral foundation of their church in China.

In the ninety years after 1860, hundreds of Irishmen and women worked as missionaries in China. It was an enormous number, given the country's small population – 5.8 million in 1861 and 4.46 million in 1901 – and the fact that China was on the other side of the world. No country was more alien and no language more difficult to learn; the Chinese government and large sections of the population were strongly against the presence of these bizarre-looking people and their strange ideas. Many Chinese called them *yang guizi* (洋鬼子), Western devils, and their Chinese converts (二洋鬼子, *er yangguizi*) "secondary Western devils". But such was the fervour of the Irish priests, nuns, pastors and doctors that they were ready to take on this great challenge; they devoted their adult life to this strange and remote country.

Making it even more difficult was the fact that many missionaries chose to live in areas outside the main cities; they had no foreign consul nor foreign soldiers to protect them or hospitals to treat their diseases. Over the 100 years from 1858, many Irish missionaries paid with their lives because of this remoteness, from disease or attack. One was Robert Warren Stewart, a graduate of Trinity College, Dublin and a member of the Church Missionary Society. He arrived in Fuzhou, southeast China in November 1876 to begin his service. On August 1, 1895, he, his wife, two of their children and seven other missionaries were murdered in Kucheng, Fujian province by members of an anti-Christian sect called the Vegetarians. Two of their other children, who were saved because they were studying in Britain at that time, went on to devote their lives to teaching at Anglican schools in Hong Kong.

In the 1840s, three graduates of Trinity College, Dublin went to China as Anglican missionaries. One of them was William Armstrong Russell, who would become the first Irish bishop in China. He and three other bishops from the Church of Ireland would be key figures in founding an independent, indigenous Anglican Church in China. They were among many missionaries, especially Protestant, who saw how Chinese regarded Christianity as a "western" religion because of its connection with opium and the foreign invaders. So they wanted to create an indigenous church, in which they played an advisory, a secondary role. It would be a "Chinese church", not a foreign one.

A pioneer in evangelism was Father Edward Galvin from

Newcestown in County Cork. From 1912 to 1916, he worked with French Vincentians in Zhejiang province. This experience persuaded him that Ireland should have its own mission for China. In 1916, with the support of the Irish Bishops, he established the Missionary Society of St. Columban, dedicated to the conversion of China. In July 1917, he met Pope Benedict XV in Rome; as a result of this meeting, the Vatican allocated a mission area round the city of Hanyang on the Yangtze River in Hubei, central China. The size of Connacht, it had a population of five million. Father Galvin lived in China from 1920 until his expulsion in 1952. His order sent hundreds of Irish priests and nuns to China, where they served as teachers, nurses and doctors as well as priests. Father, later Bishop, Galvin, also built a cathedral there and established an order of Chinese nuns. The size of the mission was due in no small part to strong financial support of the faithful at home—the Mission raised 33,000 pounds in its first year alone. Such support was essential in the early years, when the Chinese congregation was small and financially weak. On October 24, 1920, Father Galvin recorded his first Chinese convert, named Patrick Joseph Wang. In 1922, the Missionary Sisters of Saint Columban was established; by 1926, its first six sisters had arrived in China.

By 1931, the Society had 64 priests in China, 40 of them in the Hanyang area. They carried out remarkable work during the Sino-Japanese War of 1937-45, organising food, shelter and refuge for thousands of the victims of the war and floods that occurred at the same time. Also working in Hanyang at that time was a Methodist medical missionary from County Cork, Doctor Sally Christine Wolfe. She arrived in China in April 1915 and went to work at a hospital in Hankou. She served in China for the next 36 years, Other Irish Methodist medical missionaries worked in China. One, Reverend Dr Robert Booth from Cork, helped to establish the Red Cross in China. Other Irish Catholic orders which served in China were the Christian Brothers and the Irish Vincentians.

In May 1986, I had the good fortune to meet Reverend Jack Weir, on his second return visit to China since his departure in 1950. He told me about the mission in Manchuria and what had happened since. "In the beginning, the mortality rate was high. One of the first missionaries died of bubonic plague, my uncle was shot dead by thieves and then they were bandits. The Boxers (an anti-Western movement in 1900) killed dozens of believers but no missionaries."

After 1945, the People's Liberation Army controlled the countryside around Shenyang, which could only be supplied by air. "We had a big garden where we could grow vegetables and potatoes. In late 1947, the Communists took the city. They took over our schools and hospitals first, hiring us as paid staff. They ignored us and the soldiers were well behaved. We feared a huge rate bill for our property, but it did not come. In 1950, I and five Scots (missionaries) left. The theological college was closed later."

The new government expelled the foreign missionaries and reorganised the Christian churches into two institutions, the Three-Self Patriotic Movement for the Protestants and the Chinese Patriotic Catholic Association for the Catholics. Both operate under government control and supervision.

"I do not feel bitterness over the Communist takeover," said Reverend Weir. "It was for the best. It has strengthened the church which has had to stand on its own feet, not under the protection of the missionaries. It was not that they closed the country off from Christianity but closed it in. The faith has spread not by public evangelising but by person to person and by attractive living. Christians have had to keep a low profile, be cautious and keep their heads down. Some recanted and others have been lynched. I have no feeling the work was wasted. I would have liked to have kept up contact. One should take the opportunity for mission work, since you do not know how long you will have it. When I went back to the Theological College (in Shenyang which reopened) in 1983, I found 52 students, lively and independent, crammed into their class."

I marvelled at his lack of bitterness and acceptance of what had happened. He once told me that, while journalists thought of the newspaper headline for the next morning, God thought in centuries. He saw the growth of the church in China in that perspective.

The 1949 revolution provoked the flight of hundreds of thousands of Chinese who did not want to live under the new regime. Among them were many Christians who feared a repeat of the treatment of religion in the Soviet Union after 1917. About 1.5 million went to Taiwan with the Nationalist Government; foreign missionaries, including Irish ones, went with them and built new churches on the island. Today about four per cent of its population are Christian – 600,000 Protestant and 300,000 Catholics. In December 1961, two Irish nuns of the Medical Missionaries of Mary founded St Mary's Hospital in Taitung in southeast Taiwan. One of the poorest regions of the island, it had a high mortality rate among new-borns. So the hospital concentrated on gynaecology in its early years, before becoming a general hospital.

Between 1945 and 1951, about 1.5 million people fled from the mainland to Hong Kong. The 2016 census found 13.5 per cent of the city's population Christian, with 480,000 Protestants and 379,000 Catholics. Many belonged to churches that had been set up in the mainland and moved to the city. Of the Irish missionaries who left the mainland and remained in the Chinese-speaking world, a majority went to Hong Kong and a minority to Taiwan. So the legacy of the Irish missionaries can be found today in all three parts of Greater China.

By the Grace of God and the Chinese government, I was able to visit Faku in the spring of 1986. As part of its reform policy, the government opened more towns and cities to foreigners; they included Faku, which had been closed for almost forty years. My wife and I hired a taxi in Shenyang, the provincial capital, for the journey north that took about two hours. At that time, there was no such thing as a "private" visit to a small town in China. The taxi dropped us off in the courtyard of the state guest house in the town where we found a committee of welcome. The officials were friendly but nervous; they had never received a Big-Nose visitor and did not know the protocol. Faku had no famous temple or other monuments to attract tourists. The visit was very moving. I was able to meet Grandfather's former cook and members of the Christian congregation. The church and school he had built in 1907 were still standing, as was the house where he lived and Father spent the first six years of his life. Most memorable was the fact that the church and congregation Grandfather established were still active, if small. So the years he had spent there had not been in vain.

Seventy years after the Irish missionaries were expelled from China, what is their legacy? According to a White Paper issued by the State Council (Cabinet) in April 2018, the country had six million Catholics, with 8,000 "clerical personnel" serving them, and 38 million Protestants, with 57,000 "clerical personnel". It had 6,000 Catholic churches and places of assembly in 98 dioceses and 60,000 Protestant church and places of assembly. "The state respects citizens' freedom to religious belief and protects their normal religious activities," it said.

Those are the state statistics. In addition, millions belong to unofficial churches, both Catholic and Protestant. It is impossible to find accurate figures for these believers. They must worship discreetly, in homes and other meeting places, out of sight of the police and neighbourhood committees. They wisely conceal their faith from their colleagues, especially if they work in the government or a state company. They must also be very careful about contact with believers outside the mainland which has not been officially approved. Likewise, Irish and other foreign priests and ministers must exercise great discretion in their contacts with these believers.

The central city of Nanjing hosts one of the largest printers of Bibles in the world. The Amity Printing Company (愛德印刷有限公司) is the largest producer of Bibles in China. It is a joint venture with the United Bible Societies, a group of 150 Bible societies around the world. In its first year, 1988, Amity printed 500,000 Bibles. Since then, it has printed more than 100 million, in Chinese and some other minority languages, as well as many other languages for export. In the mainland, they are distributed through official Protestant churches.

In 1988, the Columbans found a way back into China. That year it set up in Hong Kong the Association for International Technological, Economic and Cultural Exchange (AITECE); its aim was "to provide a medium through which Christians from other countries could assist in the modernisation of China." This meant teaching English and other foreign languages. It was the first Catholic non-government organisation (NGO) to be officially registered in the mainland since 1949. By September 1988, it had placed four teachers in different cities, three of them priests. By September 2017, it had placed 395 teachers from 17 different countries in 23 cities and provinces in the mainland. Between 1988 and 2018, five Irish Columban priests served as General Secretary of AITECE. It expanded to offices in Ireland, the United Kingdom, the Philippines and Australia. Under its aegis, 12 Columbans have worked in China as teachers. It has also set up weaving projects, to enable Chinese Catholic communities to be self-supporting.

In June 2003, the Superior General established the China Formation Committee. Its aim was "to strengthen the structures and processes of Chinese formation by creatively assisting in the formation of Chinese priests, religious Sisters, and laity, through responding to their requests and enabling them to study outside China. We hope to respond to formation needs within China by seeking out new opportunities and innovative approaches."

In early 2008, the Columban Society moved its global headquarters to Hong Kong, after ninety years in Ireland. It made this decision for several reasons – the city's closeness to present and future missionary activity: closeness to where a majority of lay missionaries were coming from: an airport with good global connections: a good living and working environment, telecommunications and widespread use of English.

To try to understand what is going on behind the official statistics, we have to rely on anecdotes. In the 2010s, a woman in her thirties in Guangzhou told me that there were 100 million Protestants in the mainland, which would be nine million more than the membership of the Communist Party. I asked her: how do you know this?

"Yes, I am sure," she said, her eyes radiant with belief.

Professor Yang Fengguang, founding director of the Center on Religion and Chinese Society at Purdue University in the U.S., has estimated the number of Protestants in China at more than 90 million.

I later visited the Nanjing Jinling Union Theological Seminary (金陵協和神學院), the largest in China for the training of Protestant ministers. I met three professors there.

"God is angry with you Westerners," one said. "You have forgotten Him. So He has left Rome and moved elsewhere."

"Where is His new home?"

"I am not sure, but probably in Asia."

I took this to mean that the church in China was growing rapidly and God wanted to be closer to it. Once I visited the Shengjing Hospital (盛京醫院) in Shenyang, the capital of Liaoning which Grandfather often visited. The hospital was unveiling a statue to Dr Dugald Stewart, a Scottish Presbyterian missionary; in 1912, he was the first principal of the Mukden (as Shenyang was then called) Medical College. It was the first foreign medical college in northeast China; today it is the Shengjing Hospital. Attending the unveiling was a group of Scottish Presbyterian ministers; their church had retained its link to the hospital. Over dinners, the ministers explained with sadness how hard it was to keep their churches at home open—shortage of funds and members, especially the young, dwindling congregations, and buildings scattered over a wide area and elderly members unwilling to close their local church buildings and unite with one another. One day we attended a service at one of Shenyang's Protestant churches, which the Presbyterians had built almost a century before. Every seat was full, the singing fervent and the belief of the participants intensive. Is that what the Nanjing professor was talking about?

One of the most famous "house church" ministers was Reverend Samuel Lam (林獻羔) of Guangzhou. He served 22 years in prison and labour camps for refusing to join the official church. One year after his release from prison in 1978, he opened a church in his house. All three floors were dedicated to religious activity, with an estimated attendance of 4,000-5,000 a week. Those who visited the house were moved by the fervour of the participants, many holding notebooks in which they wrote down the scriptures displaying on a large screen above the preacher. Lamb died on August 3, 2013, aged 88. On August 16, his funeral was held outside the Yinhe Funeral House in the city; nearly 30,000 people attended, more than for a former Communist Party chief of the city. Dozens of plain-clothes and uniformed officers watched the crowd.

One remarkable piece of evidence of this Christian fervour is Chinese churches sending missionaries abroad. According to churches and academics, there are about 1,000 such missionaries currently working outside of China, nearly all from the unofficial churches. Like Western missionaries during the colonial era, they have taken advantage of China's rapid business expansion around the globe during the last twenty years. This is driven both by the government's Belt and Road Initiative and state and private firms going to invest in the five continents of the world. Many of them work as teachers of Mandarin or in these companies, and they tend to learn local languages. They are not afraid to evangelise the peoples of Muslim countries, including Pakistan, Iraq and Egypt, despite the clear risk of persecution and terrorism. Church leaders aim to increase the number of Chinese missionaries overseas by 2030 to 20,000.

The most remarkable of these movements is "Back to Jerusalem". This is what it says on its website: "Carrying Fire into the Dark, the largest mission movement in history. We exist to help the Chinese Church fulfil the vision they have received from God to take the good news to the nations in the 1040 window. The large majority of these peoples and nations are located between China and Jerusalem. The Chinese call this missionary movement 'Back to Jerusalem' ...The vision was born among the Chinese in the 1920s. Since that time, the churches of China have strove and even suffered persecution to fulfil what they believe is their integral role in fulfilling the Great Commission."

The first group of 36 Chinese missionaries left in March 2000 for a neighbouring Buddhist country (this wording comes from the "Back to Jerusalem" website; it does not name the country). All had suffered arrest, imprisonment, beatings and torture in China for their beliefs, the website said. Since then, hundreds have followed them to countries in the Middle East, North Africa, Central Asia, the Indian subcontinent and Southeast Asia. In June 2017, two were killed in Baluchistan in Pakistan by a group believed to be affiliated to ISIS. These Chinese Christian missionaries are taking great personal risks, probably more than Grandfather and the other Irish missionaries in 19th century China. The latter faced disease, bandits and the hostility of a part of the population. Some countries in which the Chinese missionaries work ban foreign missionaries; some Islamic countries forbid the conversion of Muslims to other religions. In addition, armed terrorist and anti-foreign groups operate in many of these countries. Beijing would not send military personnel to protect missionaries who belong to an unofficial church.

Another group is the Chinese Overseas Christian Mission (COCM), based in the United Kingdom. It describes itself as "an inter-denominational mission with the objective of sharing the Good News of Jesus Christ with the Chinese Diaspora and local communities in the UK and Europe through multi-faceted ministries. It was founded by Rev. Stephen Wang in 1950. The vision then was 'Where the Chinese are, there Christ must be.'

"Over the past seventy years, it has grown substantially," the Reverend said. "The scope of our work now covers the UK and countries on the European continent. Its vision is generations of mature Chinese believers working together throughout the

UK and Europe to share the good news of Jesus Christ through Bible-believing churches which serve local communities, and win people of all nations to Christ."

I am not sure what Grandfather would make of this Chinese missionary effort. But at least, he would respect their religious devotion and willingness to go to remote, strange countries to evangelise, just as he did.

Talking with Irish President Patrick Hillery in Beijing in 1988.

11

From Shannon to Shenzhen – Ireland in China

The next stop on my Irish journey was China. After 1949, the new Communist government had closed the country to the western world; so, along with other westerners, Irish people, including the religious workers, teachers, business people and everyone else, had to leave. The door remained closed for thirty years, until the death of Chairman Mao in September 1976. After the ten catastrophic years of the Cultural Revolution, the country was on the verge of bankruptcy. Those who took power decided that they had to make a new start. I did not imagine that one of the models for their new policy was a small town in the southwest of Ireland.

One day in 1980, eight Chinese officials visited the Shannon Special Economic Zone (SEZ) in County Clare. Established in 1959, it was the first SEZ in the world, offering tax incentives and tariff reductions to attract outside investment. One of the eight was Jiang Zemin, then vice-minister of the State Imports and Exports Administration and later General Secretary of the Communist Party. The group was impressed by what they saw. They wanted to create something similar in China, a district that would attract foreign investment but be separate from the rest of the economy. The visit was one stop on a six-week study tour of

SEZs in six nations, and at the end of the tour, the group submitted a report to the State Council (Cabinet) and National People's Congress. They were on an urgent mission. The previous decade and more of the rule of Mao Tse-tung until his death in 1976 had been an economic disaster for China. The closure of universities led to a serious shortage of educated personnel. "Revolutionary committees" took over factories with little knowledge of the enterprises they were supposed to run. From the late 1960s, foreign trade had virtually stopped. After Mao died in September 1976, his associates, the Gang of Four, were soon arrested. Only after these two events were more enlightened leaders able to take power and implement rational policies. They realised how far China had fallen behind its neighbours, including Japan, South Korea, Taiwan, Hong Kong and Singapore. It urgently needed foreign capital, technology and management—which was why the Shannon experience was so useful.

SEZs were an experiment to attract these foreigners, but in a limited and controlled way. "Feeling the stones to cross the river," was the phrase coined by Deng Xiaoping, who became paramount leader in 1978. He and his colleagues wanted to retain the single-party Communist system but experiment with the economy. In 1980, they set up three SEZs in Guangdong province, in Shenzhen, Zhuhai and Shantou, and one in Fujian province, in Xiamen. Jiang served as party chief from 1989 to 2002. Many leaders followed in his footsteps to Shannon—two prime ministers, Wen Jiabao and Zhu Rongji, two vice prime ministers, Huang Ju and Zeng Peiyan, and, on February 18 2012, Xi Jinping, then vice-president and now party leader.

This is what Xi said that day to Vincent Cunnane, CEO of Shannon Development, and his guests: "Shannon Development is one of the oldest and the most successful economic development zones in the world. For decades, it not only made significant contributions to the economic development of Ireland, but also provided a useful reference for the economic development in many other countries in the world. China has learned a lot of useful experience from Shannon Development to build China's special economic zones, Shanghai Pudong New Area, Tianjin Binhai New Area and other development zones. Many Chinese delegations came to visit here to learn experience and they were deeply impressed."

Shannon and the four SEZs were milestones in the economies of Ireland and China; both followed a policy of "reform" and "open-door". Like the leaders of China after Mao, the leaders of Ireland in the 1960s wanted a drastic change in economic policy. After independence in 1922, the Fianna Fail government aimed for an economy based on agriculture that was largely self-sufficient. It was not a success. Tens of thousands emigrated; while politically independent, the country remained an economic colony of Britain. In the 1960s, Prime Minister Sean Lemass initiated tax breaks and grants to foreign firms setting up in Ireland and abolished protectionist assistance given to domestic firms. This open-door policy and low rate of corporate tax have been the basis of the economic success of Ireland ever since. By 1973, foreign firms accounted for almost one third of manufacturing employees in the country. The success of China since 1980 has been even more spectacular. It has become the world's second-largest economy, after the United States. Shannon is more than 10,000 kilometres from Shenzhen, so it is remarkable that it was able to play a role in the economic miracle that has transformed city since 1980.

Deng's market reforms reversed many (but certainly not all) of the policies Mao had instituted thirty years before. Mao expelled all the foreigners, including the missionaries; he only allowed the entry of a small number of experts and teachers, mainly from the Soviet bloc. The split with the West widened after he sent Chinese troops to fight on the northern side in the Korean War in October 1950; as a reprisal, the United States and its allies set up a trade embargo against China. The rift lasted until January 1, 1979 when the two countries established diplomatic relations. From the early 1980s, Irish people were, like other Westerners, able to live and work in China, with the necessary visas. The government gave them to investors, employees of multinational companies, financial institutions, teachers, lawyers, journalists and students – but no missionaries. Ireland established diplomatic relations with China on June 22, 1979. Its first ambassador in China, John Campbell, presented his credentials on May 17, 1980. That year, the embassy in Beijing moved to its current site. Setting up ties was a wise decision. At that time, business, personal and cultural links between the two countries were negligible. But Dublin saw that China was opening up and would become a major diplomatic player in Asia. Ireland was outward-looking and trade-focused; China could become a major export market. At that time, few Chinese even knew where Ireland was. They could, however, name the country – 愛爾蘭 (Ai Er Lan), which means Love and Orchids. China is usually polite in naming big countries, calling France the Country of Law (法國, *faguo*), Germany the Country of Morality (德國, *deguo*), the U.S. the Country of Beauty (美國, *meiguo*) and the UK the Country of the Brave (英國, *yingguo*). For smaller countries, China tends to use an entirely phonetic approach to the choice of characters used for the name.

When I asked Chinese people to name an Irish person, they could not. The first to enter the public consciousness were players in the English Premier League, broadcast live in China to tens of millions from the 1990s. Manchester United was one of the most popular teams, so Roy Keane and Denis Irwin became familiar.

My own name in Chinese, (should be Ao, thanks for correction) Ao-ni-er (奧尼爾), was instantly forgettable until Yao Ming, China's most successful basketball player, moved in 2002 to the Houston Rockets in the National Basketball Association (NBA); at 2.29 metres, he was the tallest player in the NBA. The best player in the league then was Shaquille O'Neal, 2.16 metres tall, with the Los Angeles Lakers. Games between the two teams were carried live on Chinese television; Au-ni-er became a household name. "Oh yes, we know your name," Chinese would say.

In the 1980s, the new foreign residents were, like Deng, "feeling the stones to cross the river". China had been cut off from the world for three decades; contact between Chinese and foreigners had been strictly controlled. The open-door policy eased the restrictions, but neither side knew what the limits were. Each was intensely curious about the other. But were some topics not to be discussed? Was someone nearby recording the conversation? Was dating allowed, and was it a risk to the Chinese partner? There was also something that seems to have always existed in all Socialist countries – the gap between "reality" and "Socialist reality". That is to say, there was an official version, which may or may not accord with reality. Here is one example. In 1980, an Irish lady named Mary joined an official tour of south China; the last stop was Guangzhou. The guide was a charming man named Li; he took the group around a lake. Mary was getting on well with Mr Li; since the tour was about to end, she felt she could ask him a personal question. "Do you have children, Mr Li?" There was a long pause. That year China introduced a one-child policy, limiting couples to a single child. Under Mao, there had been no population control; it nearly doubled from 540 million in 1949 to 969 million in 1979. Mr Li thought for a long time and then answered: "One or two." With the new policy, the official answer to the question was "one"; but Mr Li did not want to lie to this friendly visitor – so he found a way to cover both bases.

In the 1980s, China was still a poor country and foreign exchange in short supply. Since going abroad meant spending U.S. dollars, it was limited to official delegations; they were given only the amount they needed for hotels, meals and travel. There was no tourism by Chinese individuals. Close to the Irish embassy in Beijing was the Friendship Store, which sold imported goods such as televisions, radios, refrigerators and foreign food; all had been purchased with foreign currency, so the buyer had to pay in it too. The central bank started issuing a special money for foreigners called Foreign Exchange Certificates (FECs) in 1980; they could use the FECs in the Friendship Store. But it was off-limits to ordinary residents who could only stand outside and watch, with anger and wonderment, at the privileged foreigners coming out with their Sony televisions and Panasonic tape recorders. In legal terms, the FEC was at parity with the national currency, the renminbi (RMB). But, in reality, there was a black market, since the FEC enabled you to buy imported goods, and the rate varied between 1.2 and 1.7. Foreigners could change their FECs into renminbi; the problem was where to spend it. Hotels, shops and restaurants catering for foreigners would only accept FECs, not renminbi. So foreigners went to shops and restaurants catering for Beijing residents; they were happy to accept renminbi. The FECs were finally abandoned in 1994.

How the world has turned on its head since then. Chinese tourists have become the world's biggest spenders, with a record of US$277 billion in 2018, more than double the Americans in second place. Countries that were in the 1980s reluctant to give tourist visas to individual Chinese are today falling over themselves to do so. For me, the moment of awakening of this new world came one Sunday summer morning in Paris in 2011.

Strolling with my wife from Hong Kong along the Champs Elysees, we came to the flagship store of Louis Vuitton; it is one of the brands most favoured by Chinese. On the pavement outside were Parisian residents, Big-Noses like me, as well as blacks and Arabs. Peering through the windows, we saw that nearly all those inside were people with black hair. On the door stood two burly guards, whose job was to keep out people who were curious but appeared to have no money to spend. Fortunately, my black-haired, Asian-featured wife qualified; she entered and I squeezed in behind her. It was as if we had left Europe. Nearly all the clients were Chinese, as well as a few Koreans and Japanese. Many of the staff spoke Mandarin, including Chinese residents of Paris, Chinese students and French people who had learnt it. On the second floor, we met a young salesman from Taiwan. He told us he was studying engineering in Paris and worked in the shop at the weekends. We could not afford to buy anything, of course, but it was eye-opening.

The next day we had a similar experience. We went to Galeries Lafayette, an up-market department store popular with Chinese visitors. Immediately after we entered, two elegant saleswomen rushed forward and introduced themselves to my wife: "What are you looking for?" one said. "We have VIP rooms where you can look at items in peace and quiet."

They whisked her away, leaving the gormless husband behind. Wandering around the shop, I marvelled at the lovely goods and chatted to the staff. Well-trained, they knew quickly whether I would spend anything; they did not waste much time. To save face, I bought a small bar of soap for 10 euros as a gift. It was the opposite of the Beijing Friendship Store thirty years before.

Ireland is one of the many countries that have benefitted from the arrival of Chinese tourists. In 2019, the last pre-Covid year,

110,000 visited the island, up from 55,000 in 2016. Tourism Ireland aims to attract 220,000 by 2025; each year, again pre-Covid, about four million Chinese visited Europe. This rapid growth was a result of intensive marketing, in print, digital and social media. In May 2019, Tourism Ireland's largest-ever sales mission to China, with 26 tourism businesses, visited four cities; they met hundreds of travel agents and tour operators, key airlines and travel journalists. In June 2018, Cathay Pacific started flying directly from Hong Kong to Dublin, with four flights a week. It was the first route between Dublin and an Asian city. For the Irish tourism industry at the time, it was a "game-changer".

For Chinese visitors, the three top attractions in Ireland are the Giant's Causeway, the Titanic Museum in Belfast and the Guinness Storehouse in Dublin. In 2017, the Storehouse attracted 50,000 Chinese, out of the total of 1.7 million total visitors. Other attractions are Ireland's 500 golf courses: landscape and hiking along the Cliffs of Moher: music and dance: and shopping.

The most prominent Irish entrepreneur in China is Liam Casey, founder and CEO of PCH (Pacific Coast Highway), with corporate headquarters in Cork, operational headquarters in Shenzhen and U.S. headquarters in San Francisco; it has annual turnover of more than US$1 billion. He was one of the first Irish businessmen to see the opportunity to match Chinese manufacturing with western markets; none has been so successful. PCH has ten regional offices and employs more than 5,000 staff of more than sixteen nationalities in seven countries.

Casey was born in 1966 in a dairy farm in Donoughmore, County Cork. His first ten working years were in retail. He helped set up Meadows and Byrne and ended up running the Club Tricot line for Blarney Woollen Mills. At Club Tricot, he bought all the materials in France and Germany and had the clothes made in Ireland and delivered to the retail stores. "It was all about timing, you never wanted stock to run out in any of the stores, but at the same time you never wanted too much inventory. Quality had to be perfect and it involved huge co-ordination."

It proved to be excellent training for his present career. In 1995, he went to California and, in the following year, set up PCH with US$20,000, to source computer components from Taiwan for the growing number of U.S. manufacturers setting up in Ireland; this would cut out the traditional UK and European distributors. After a 10-day visit to Taiwan, he persuaded AST, a computer company, to give him his first contract. Business grew so rapidly that his Taiwan supplier built a new factory in Dongguan in Guangdong province. He himself went to Guangdong and ended up spending much of his time there. He developed an intimate knowledge of the province's suppliers and what they made. He promised delivery of a product from Guangdong to a consumer anywhere in the world in two days. PCH masterminded the design, manufacture and distribution of hardware from the initial online order to the delivery to the customer's door, anywhere in the world. PCH made a breakthrough in 1999, when Apple hired him as a supplier.

In 2003, Casey opened a packaging facility in Shenzhen and then a fulfilment centre. His client base grew to include large Chinese companies as well as multinationals. He spent many days flying between Shenzhen, San Francisco and Cork. By 2012, PCH had revenues of US$815 million.

According to his company's website, he has lived 23 years in China. "He is recognised as a thought leader in strategic sourcing, new product introductions, supply chain management, sustainability and start-up initiatives.,. We provide the supply chain visibility and predictability that allows our customers to best manage their business." It said that Europe accounted for 43 per cent of its deliveries, followed by Asia with 34 per cent and North America with 22 per cent. Its customers include Beats, Apple and many other household brand names. The products include tablet computers, e-readers, PCs, accessories and other electronic products.

"I chose this lifestyle, the energy, the adrenalin rush I get from Shenzhen," he said. "It is huge. It is the sense of excitement and wonder of this place. The pace of change and progress – there is nowhere like it in the world." (note: looked on company website. It does not say impact of Covid on the firm or where Casey has lived during Covid. Suggest we avoid the issue) ination."

Another Irish legacy in China is the *Titanic*, the ship launched in Belfast in May 1911. Its story and the 1997 film directed by James Cameron captured the imagination of many Chinese, none more so than Su Shaojun, an entrepreneur in the central province of Sichuan. He sold his assets in the energy industry to invest one billion renminbi (US$155 million) in a 100 percent replica of what was the world's largest ship when it was launched from a Northern Ireland shipyard in 1912. It is a most ambitious project. The dining room, the luxury, cabins and even the door handles use the style of the original; it will have a functioning steam engine. It is 269 metres long and 28 metres wide. It is designed to have dining rooms, first-, second- and third-class cabins, Turkish baths, a gymnasium and swimming pool, and a Grand Staircase. It is designed to accommodate 2,400 passengers and 900 staff. The great ship is supposed for form the centrepiece of a theme park in Daying county (大英縣) in a reservoir on the Qijiang river in Sichuan province; it is more than 1,000 km from the sea.

Asked the rationale for such a Pharaohonic project, Su said: "People have never forgotten how at that time people sacrificed their lives to carry out their responsibilities, with men protecting the women and children and couples side by side in life and death. That is the Titanic spirit of responsibility and universal love. Let it become the place to pass on and experience the great spirit of Titanic."

As of 2022, it was unclear if the project would ever be completed. Images taken from the air in 2021 showed that construction had stopped.

In April 2021, the world learnt the sad story of the eight Chinese aboard the *Titanic*. They were recounted by a British director, Arthur Jones, in a documentary film "The Six" (六人), about the six who survived. The eight boarded the ship at Southampton with third-class tickets, each costing 56 pounds, nine shillings and 11 pence. They were among the 704 passengers in third class. After a stop in Queenstown (Cobh), the ship sailed for New York and hit the iceberg on the night of April 14. The eight Chinese escaped from the sinking ship; two drowned, but the other six were able to reach lifeboats or float on driftwood until rescue ships picked them up. Of the 2,224 crew and passengers on board, only 705 survived. The boats carried the survivors to the Port of New York—but, because of laws excluding Chinese from the United States, the six were not allowed entry, except Chip Chang who was sick. He was admitted for hospital treatment; two years later, he died in London.

George Bernard Shaw, one of four Irish writers to win the Nobel Prize for literature, visited Shanghai for one day—less than 24 hours on February 17, 1933. He was invited to a lunch with two of China's most prominent intellectuals, Tsai Yuen-pei and Lu Hsun (Lu Xun). His host was Song Ching-ling, widow of Sun Yat-sen, first President of the Republic of China established after the Xinhai Revolution in October 1911. She hosted the event at her home in Rue Molière in the French Concession. It and the neighbouring International Concessions were under the control of foreign powers; the Chinese government had no authority over them. Because of this, many Chinese preferred to live in them, beyond the writ of their own government. Early that February morning, Madame Sun took a boat to the anchorage of the passenger vessel *Empress of Britain*, picked up GBS from it and brought him to her house for lunch.

I think Shaw probably didn't realise how privileged he was to meet these three Chinese individuals. Tsai was the single most important figure in modernising China's education system after the overthrow of the Qing dynasty. He was President of Beijing University and, in 1928, helped to found Academia Sinica, the country's most important research institution. Lu Hsun was the most prominent Chinese novelist of the Republican period (1911-49). Madame Sun belonged to one of the most powerful families in China. One sister married President Chiang Kai-shek and another Kung Hsiang-hsi, who served as Vice-Premier and Premier. He was an extremely wealthy man. If Shaw wanted to understand China in the 1930s, he could not have asked for three better interlocutors. But, from what we know of the meeting, the three Chinese were extremely polite and invited GBS to talk, which he was happy to do. So they learnt more about him than vice versa. Lu and radical writers like him admired the work of the Irish literary revival, especially its fight against oppression and desire for a new national spirit. The works of Oscar Wilde and J.M. Synge were available in China in translation. Lady Gregory's The Rising of the Moon and Cathleen Ni Houlihan of W.B. Yeats and Lady Gregory were performed in theatres and universities. In 1936, Juno and the Paycock played to packed houses in Shanghai.

Lu died in October 1936, aged 55, and Tsai died in March 1940, aged 72. When the Communists established the People's Republic in 1949, Song Ching-ling remained on the mainland;

she went on to hold senior positions in the government, including "Honorary President" during her final illness in May 1981. She never re-married. In 1949, her two sisters went with the Nationalist government to Taiwan. The Chinese conclusion about the three, from the perspective of the new government at least, was that one loved power, one loved money and the other loved the country.

In April 2003, I also had the great good fortune to meet GBS in Shanghai, only virtually as he had died in 1950. This was thanks to Irish Consul-General Geoffrey Keating who organised a week of events to mark the 70th anniversary of the visit. He invited distinguished Irish professors to speak at the Blarney Stone, the city's leading Irish public house. One was Professor Nicholas Grene, head of the English department at Trinity College. He gave a talk on Shaw's complex identity, both Irish and British. I was enthralled. I realised that, for the first time, I was listening to a detailed analysis of my own father. The professor quoted Shaw as saying: "I have lived for 20 years in Ireland and for 72 in England. But the 20 came first, and in Britain, I am still a foreigner and shall die one."

Shaw's talent and fame enable him to move easily among Irish and British society. He was comfortable in his skin and retained his Irish accent. But that was not the case for Father, nor for thousands of other Irish people in Britain. They had to bear the prejudice and slights, said or unsaid, aimed at them and to negotiate the obstacle course of the British class system. Shaw was able to describe this in meticulous and humorous detail and make British, and foreign, audiences laugh at them. Father had to live within this system. The quote on his childhood did not apply to Father. His first twenty years were not so happy, not Shaw's cottage on Dalkey Hill with its view of the Wicklow Mountains and Killiney Bay. I picture those twenty years for

Father as the modest kitchens and living rooms of the Belfast homes where he lived and the classrooms and sports fields of RBAI and Queens. They were materially comfortable and gave him the privilege of an excellent education; but they were, I think, cold and strictly disciplined. After he moved to England, he did not want to return; he used all his energy to adapt to the new society to which he wished to belong. He made a successful career as a psychiatrist, which he could never have done in Belfast or Dublin. But, as with Shaw, Father's Irish personality lived on in the new setting. He was charming and humorous; but he was different to those around him. I thank Professor Grene for helping me understand Father.

Another lecturer Geoffrey Keating invited to the Blarney Stone was Terence Dolan, Professor of Old and Middle English at University College. He spoke about Hiberno-English, especially the influence of Gaelic words on the English language used in Ireland. My education included years of classical Greek and Latin but, unfortunately, no Irish. So Dolan's lecture explained many things, including words which I had heard and often used but whose origin I did not know. The words and expressions came from Gaelic; they had created a different language. Each year on June 16, Geoffrey organised events to mark Bloomsday, the day on which James Joyce and his novel *Ulysses* are celebrated, with readings and talks at different venues. Thanks to him and other Irish diplomats, I have heard readings in Mandarin, Shanghainese, Cantonese, Korean, Japanese, French, Gaelic and other languages—is *Ulysses* the "global novel"?

Another highlight of Shanghai was the visit by President Mary McAleese to the city in October 2003. It was her first visit to China since becoming president in 1997. At the Garden Hotel in Shanghai, she made a speech at an education round table.

"Ireland is not as remote as it might at first seem, for here in

China, great Irish names are already well known—Joyce, Yeats, George Bernard Shaw, Beckett, more latterly Seamus Heaney and the young people will have heard of U2, Westlife and the Corrs,: she said. "Over the past ten years, the number of full-time students in third-level education has increased by almost eighty per cent. Half the Irish workforce has experience third-level education. And sixty per cent of Ireland's third-level students major in engineering, science or business studies. There has been a welcome growth in student numbers from China studying at Irish universities and institutes of technology. On their return to China, they will no doubt play an important role in building the Chinese economy in the 21st century."

During her visit, the consulate arranged a large reception at the Garden Hotel. It is a building full of history. Before World War Two, the area had been part of the French Concession. In 1903, the Germans built their Recreation Club on the site of the hotel. The building was confiscated in 1918; in 1924, it became the French Chamber of Commerce. During World War Two, the Japanese army occupied it; after their defeat, it was the American Naval Club. In 1985, Nomura Securities financed the construction of a five-star hotel with 470 rooms adjoined to the old club.

To meet a president, it was necessary to buy a gift—traditional Chinese music, I thought. So I went out and purchased three tapes of such music. Like everyone else, we bought fake tapes and discs for our music and films. Nearby our apartment was a young lady from Anhui in central China with a large stall; over time, she learnt our tastes and acquired French, Swedish and other European films for us, about US$1 per disc; so our evening entertainment was very rich. I showed the tapes to my wife for her approval.

"Oh, no," she said. "You cannot give counterfeit products to a head of state. You will have to buy the genuine items."

So I went to the official music shop; there was no-one there except the staff. I bought the same three tapes for five times the price of the fakes.

The reception was a grand affair, with hundreds of guests, Chinese and foreign. I queued up to meet President McAleese, a charismatic lady. I bowed and presented the gifts. We exchanged a few words; I cherished her lovely smile. For a few brief seconds, I was the centre of her magic gaze. Then it was time to mingle. I walked up to a white couple in late middle age.

"Where do you come from?" they asked.

"Born in England to an Irish father and educated in England," I said. "I am working in Shanghai now."

"No, no, we do not believe you," said the wife; she had the accent of the British upper class, full of contempt. She did not believe my account of myself, that I was born and educated in England.

I wondered what to do: stay and argue with them? No, not worth it, especially at such a happy event. So I went to talk to a group of Chinese people; that was much more relaxing. Meeting such a couple was a reminder of the obstacles Father had faced in the UK in the 1950s and 1960s.

In 2020, Ireland exported to China goods worth 10.56 billion euros, an increase of 18.25 per cent over 2019; imports from China rose 18.52 per cent to 6.21 billion euros. That made China the country's largest trade partner in Asia and fifth largest overall. Ireland is one of the few Western countries with a trade surplus with China. Chinese firms have invested more than one billion euros in Ireland, creating nearly 1,000 jobs. Going the other way, more than ninety Irish companies have invested in China, with about 10,000 jobs.

None of the Irish and Chinese officials who met during that visit to Shannon SEZ in 1980 could have imagined such an outcome. Bilateral trade then was only a few million U.S. dollars; neither country was a significant investor overseas. This dramatic growth is the result of the economic 'miracles' in both countries in the forty years since. For the first two decades, both relied for their growth on substantial amounts of inward investment. During the second two decades, their economies had grown to the point that they could export capital.

Ireland has greatly benefitted from a revolution in the Chinese diet since 1980, especially the consumption of dairy products and, with higher incomes, the willingness to buy premium, imported food. In 2020, the country exported 872 million euros of food products to China, its fourth largest market for such goods. It was the second largest for dairy and pigmeat. Other food exports are beef, seafood and spirits. The most important food export is infant formula; Ireland accounts for about ten per cent of the Chinese market. Its farmers compete fiercely with those of Holland, New Zealand, Germany, France and Denmark; these six countries accounted for 90 per cent of Chinese imports of infant formula in 2020. The foreign producers have greatly benefitted from a scandal in 2008 in which six babies died and 300,000 fell ill from ingesting domestic infant formula that contained melamine, a chemical used in the production of plastics, cement and fertilizer. This persuaded millions of Chinese mothers to shun local brands and buy imported ones, despite the higher cost.

Irish brands such as Kerrygold butter and cheese, Avonmore milk and SuperValu own-brands are available in Chinese supermarkets in major cities, as well as online. Guinness, Jameson and Baileys are also on sale in bars and supermarkets. This share of the Chinese market was not won easily. It required intensive marketing by the companies and engagement by Irish officials with their Chinese counterparts; the food sector is tightly regulated.

Two images greatly helped this growth. One was a photograph of Xi Jinping, then a member of the Politburo but not yet Party leader, kicking a Gaelic football in Croke Park on February 19, 2012, in front of a group of admiring Irish officials. He was on a three-day visit to Ireland, his second since 2003. He attended an Ireland-China trade forum in Dublin involving about 300 companies. A keen football fan, Xi is said to keep this photograph on his desk, next to those of his wife and daughter. The other image was that of Premier Li Keqiang and his wife having tea with Cathal Garvey and his family on their farm in Ower, County Mayo, on May 17, 2015. The farm, with 110 Holstein/Freisian dairy cows, covers 109 hectares and has been in the Garvey family for more than 250 years. Taoiseach Enda Kenny and his wife accompanied the visitors. Cathal served his guests with home-made bread, cheese and milk and explained his crop cultivation, agro-processing and quality control. Li's visit was widely covered in the Chinese media – the publicity was worth 1,000 advertisements, especially to assure consumers in China on the safety and quality of Irish food.

My years in China provided an opportunity to meet many Irish people, including diplomats, business people, accountants, lawyers and teachers. I don't believe I met any missionaries, but you could not be sure. People said that religious orders send staff to live and work in China with other identities, such as teacher or technical specialist. They do their evangelisation with discretion and do not admit to it openly.

The Irish diplomats were most warm and helpful. In May 1988, President Patrick Hillery went to Beijing on an official visit; the embassy arranged a reception one evening. That afternoon one of the staff called to say that they did not have enough guests and asked me to find more.

"Must they be Irish?" I said.

"More or less," he said. "We are flexible on this."

So I worked the phones, asking everyone I knew with an Irish connection—and some without—if they could attend. In the event, there was a good turnout. The President looked happy enough with the welcome he received—the Irish family expanded for the evening!

At the Yasukuni Shrine in Tokyo.

12

Ireland in Japan

The next stop on my journey was Japan, where we arrived at Christmas in 1989. I knew that Irish missionaries had gone there but was hazy about the rest of the story between the two countries. I had only been in Tokyo six months when I discovered that James Joyce had been, in spirit, an early arrival.

It was a summer evening; I was invited to the apartment of an Irish diplomat. The occasion was to meet translators of James Joyce's *Ulysses*. The three well-dressed men were Saiichi Maruya, Reiji Nagakawa and Yuichi Takamatsu. I could not conceal my admiration and astonishment at their work. The book is hard to follow in English; how much more difficult – if not impossible – to render it into a foreign language? As I talked to the three men, I realised how far I was behind the curve. Theirs was the fifth translation into Japanese. The first was in 1931, the third in the world after German in 1927 and French in 1929. That meant that the Japanese public could read a legal copy of the book three years before Americans, six years before the British and 30 years before the Irish. The first article about Joyce in Japan, on his book *A Portrait of the Artist as a Young Man*, appeared in a magazine in March 1918.

I took two things away from that evening. One was the intense interest of Japanese in foreign things, especially from the West. The other was their diligence and meticulousness in studying them. The five translations of *Ulysses* were one example of this. Another was everything around us in Tokyo – the cars, the state-of-the-art electronics and the skyscrapers that could withstand earthquakes. During the final years of World War Two, Allied bombing raids devastated Japanese cities – half of Tokyo was leveled to the ground. In Japan's three largest cities, Tokyo, Osaka and Nagoya, the bombing reduced 260 square kilometres of urban area to rubble. After Emperor Hirohito surrendered on August 15 1945, Japan had to rebuild from almost zero. We arrived at the end of 1989, just 44 years later, and in that short time, it had become the most advanced economy in Asia exporting its products all over the world. That was the result of the education and hard work of millions of people like the three professors.

Japan is 9,500 kilometres from Ireland, the country furthest from it in Asia; it has never allowed mass immigration. Nonetheless, Irish people have left their mark on this place so far away. The oldest record of an Irish person going there dates to July 1704, when a sailor named Robert Jansen, from Waterford, was captured off the coast of Kyushu. He and five companions had escaped from the Dutch East India Company in the Philippines and set sail in a small boat hoping to reach the port of Canton, now known in English as Guangzhou. The six were taken prisoner and held for four months on suspicion of being Portuguese missionaries. In November 1704, they were released and put on a Dutch ship bound for Batavia, now Jakarta, in the Dutch East Indies. Jansen arrived during the "closed-country" period between 1639 and 1853. Almost no foreigners were allowed entry, nor Japanese to leave.

On July 8, 1853, an American naval commander named Matthew Perry brought his vessels to Uraga, at the entrance of Tokyo Bay, and compelled the government to allow American and other Western countries to trade with Japan. It was the country's great good fortune that many Japanese saw Perry's arrival as a warning that their homeland could follow India, Indochina, Indonesia and other countries in Asia and become a colony of a Western power. In 1868, a group of reformers overthrew the government and took power in what is known as the Meiji Restoration. Acutely aware of how far they were behind the developed world, they sent people to Europe and the United States to learn the skills and languages of industry, science, medicine, education and modern armaments. Their giant neighbour China faced the identical threat. But the Qing dynasty of the Manchus did not heed the warnings; ignoring the advice of Chinese and foreign reformers, it did not modernise. In 1894-95, a modern Japanese navy built in little over twenty years wiped out the Chinese fleet. In the peace treaty that followed, the Qing court had to pay an indemnity of 200 million taels (8,000 metric tonnes) of silver and cede the island of Taiwan in perpetuity.

One outcome of the Meiji Restoration was permission for foreign military personnel to be based in Japan. In 1868, the British 10th Foot Regiment, First Battalion, arrived, to protect the small foreign community in Yokohama. Among them was bandmaster John William Fenton, born in Kinsale, County Cork in March 1828. Japanese naval cadets heard his band rehearsing and persuaded Fenton to become their instructor, and this became the first Japanese brass band.Fenton ordered instruments for them from London. In 1869, he realised that Japan had no national anthem and needed one. He worked with an artillery captain who chose a 10-century poem for the words. He asked Fenton to write the music, which he did. It was performed in front of Emperor Meiji when he inspected the troops in 1870. His music became the first version of "Kimigayo" (君が代) which has ever since been the Japanese national anthem, surviving even the defeat of World War Two. After 1945, Germany had to write a new anthem. The anthem we hear today includes part of Fenton's original music.

When his battalion left Japan in 1871, Fenton stayed for a further six years as a bandmaster with the newly formed Japanese navy and then the band of the Imperial court.

Another Irishman who made a great contribution in the early years of the Meiji era was engineer and architect Thomas James Waters from Birr, County Offaly. He lived in Japan from 1864 to 1877 and designed the Imperial Mint in Osaka, and a military barracks and the Ginza Bricktown in Tokyo. After the Ginza district was devastated by fire in 1872, he designed a new modern street plan, with two-storey Gregorian brick buildings similar to those of Dublin. The plan is visible today and Ginza remains one of the most important shopping districts in Japan's capital.

It was during this period of intense foreign learning that the first Japanese came to Ireland. A mission led by Tomomi Iwakura visited Europe and U.S. from 1871 to 1873. During their stay in England from August to December 1872, the deputy leader of the mission, Takayoshi Kodi, and three other members visited Dublin on December 3 1872. They visited the Guinness brewery where they sampled a pint of the famous brew. This was probably the first visit by a representative of the Japanese government to Ireland.

The new government after 1868 welcomed foreigners like Fenton and Waters, as long as they could help the country's modernisation. Among them were many Irish priests and nuns, and hundreds have lived and worked in Japan since the start of the Meiji era. Their greatest contribution has been in education, a vital piece of the transformation from a feudal system to a modern state. The earliest foreign institution was Saint Maur's in Yokohama; the first international school in Japan, it opened in 1872 and is flourishing today. This was founded by the Sisters of the Holy Infant Jesus, a French order. In 1901, it founded Futaba Gakuen for local girls.

During the early decades of the 20th century, hundreds of Irish men and women joined religious orders. For the women, it was an alternative to a restricted married life, and a way to continue education and join a respected career. Seeking teachers and missionaries for East Asia, the Sisters of the Holy Infant Jesus set up Drishane Convent in 1909 in Millstreet, County Cork. Among the early novitiates was Mary Angela Fitzgerald, who had earlier qualified as a teacher. In 1919, the order sent her to St Maur's. She was attending morning Mass on September 1, 1923 at the school church when Yokohama was devastated by the worst earthquake ever to hit Japan, measuring 7.9 on the Richter scale. A total of 140,000 people died, including the priest and 234 of the 235 people attending his Mass; only Sister Angela survived. She and her fellow Sisters rebuilt the school. In 1938, Hidesaburo Shoda, president of the Nisshin Flour Milling Company, asked Sister Angela to teach English to his five-year-old daughter, named Michiko. She agreed; she introduced her three nephews and nieces in Ballybunnion, County Kerry as pen-pals for the young Japanese girl. An outstanding student, Michiko graduated summa cum laude from the University of the Sacred Heart, a Catholic university in Tokyo, with a B.A. in English Literature. She was also a gifted pianist. In August 1957 occurred a meeting that changed her life. She was playing tennis on a court at Karuizawa near Nagano, when she met Crown Prince Akihito, the future Emperor. They fell in love and married on April 10, 1959. She was the first woman outside the nobility to marry into the Imperial family. He ascended to the throne on

January 7, 1989. Sister Angela died aged 90 on July 26, 1980 and is buried in the cemetery of her order in Yokohama. In September 2005, Empress Michiko paid a state visit to Ireland with her husband. In an interview, she said that she had been taught by Irish nuns and recalled "the charm and loveliness of each one of them." She speaks Irish with some fluency.

Another Irish nun had a lifelong attachment to St Maur's School. In 1947, Sister Carmel O'Keeffe, from Cork, was sent to Yokohama to reopen the school after the war. She served there for sixty years, including as principal from 1967 to 1991. She died in her home city of Cork on October 17, 2011, aged 93.

Empress Michiko was an important figure during the four years that my wife Louise and I spent in Japan, working as a reporter and editor for Reuters news agency. Circumstances could not have been kinder to me. In September 1985, the finance ministers and central bank governors of the U.S., France, Germany, Britain and Japan met at the Plaza Hotel in New York. They agreed to an "orderly appreciation of non-dollar currencies". This led to a dramatic appreciation of the yen and the value of Japan's assets rose suddenly. Reuters greatly benefitted from this – and had an ample budget to give expats like me generous allowances. Louise and I picked an apartment in Roppongi in central Tokyo; it was so close to the office that I could cycle to work. I soon discovered that most of my Japanese colleagues had a one-way commute of one hour or more on a crowded train or subway. I tried to avoid mentioning where I lived; when they learnt of it, you could feel their sense of injustice.

The Imperial family became an important story. Naruhito, eldest son of the emperor who had ascended to the throne in January 1989, had no wife; his first duty was to marry and have a son to succeed him. The lady he yearned for was Masako Owada, the daughter of a senior diplomat. She had grown up in Moscow and New York and, back in Tokyo, attended the Catholic Futaba Gakuen school set up by the French and Irish nuns. In 1986, she was one of 28 people, only two of them women, out of 800 applicants to enter the Ministry of Foreign Affairs. With her knowledge of foreign languages and global personal network, she had ahead of her a stellar career, a woman pioneer in a bureaucracy dominated by men. Unwilling to give up this future, she refused the advances of the royal prince. The Japanese media was reporting this story breathlessly then, suddenly, it disappeared from the news. A Japanese colleague told me that the Imperial Household Agency (IHA) had summoned editors of newspapers and television stations and "asked" them, in the "the national interest", to self-censor the story for six months. This would give the two time and space for their courtship, it said. When Miss Owada still did not agree, this period was extended for a further three months. Then, on the afternoon of January 19 1992, my telephone rang—a friend at a major newspaper. "Whatever schedule you have this evening, cancel it," he said. "Be at home in front of a television at 1900. You will learn everything about Miss Masako."

I followed his advice. At 7 p.m., I tuned in—all the channels announced the engagement and had detailed coverage of her life and interviews with her relatives, friends and teachers. She had finally accepted his proposal the previous December 9—giving the channels a month to prepare their programmes. The episode showed that the Imperial family enjoyed a privilege and protection from the media that the British royal family had also historically enjoyed, until it lost it during the era of Princess Diana in the 1980s.

Miss Owada—since May 2019 the Empress of Japan—was right to be fearful to enter the ultra-conservative Imperial Palace. She had her first pregnancy in 1999, but miscarried. The couple had one daughter, born in December 2001, after eight years of marriage. Between 2004 and 2014, she was largely out of the public eye, receiving medical treatment. People believe this was due to the pressure of having to produce a male heir, criticism from IHA officials who did not like a "modern woman" as the Princess and adjusting to a life filled with so many arcane rules. Our Japanese lady friends saw her story as a metaphor for the restrictions they faced in professional and social life. Miss Owada had the skills and connections to become a future ambassador or representative of Japan at the United Nations—but had to give this up "in the national interest". Her best friend in the Palace was said to be Princess Michiko, educated by Irish nuns; she, too, was an intelligent and well-educated outsider who had to learn to live within this straightjacket.

The nearest I came to the Imperial family was a lavish St Patrick's Day dinner at which Phil Coulter performed. The guest of honour was Princess Akishino, wife of the younger brother of Naruhito and sister-in-law of Miss Owada. She gave an excellent speech in English. She had a similar profile to her sister-in-law. The daughter of an academic, she grew up abroad; she is highly educated and earned a Ph.D degree. She and her husband have two daughters and one son. From what we could see, she adjusted better to life within the Imperial family—perhaps because, unlike Miss Owada, she was not married to the heir of the throne, and she did not live in the main palace in central Tokyo. That evening Coulter played "The Town I Loved So Well", his native city of Derry; it is the most memorable of the many songs of the Troubles. His rendering brought the house down.

Once a year, the Emperor gave a news conference. This was very formal, with only a limited range of topics. He was not allowed by law to speak about politics. The IHA carefully vetted reporters before letting them take part. First, it had to be sure they would follow the rules and, second, know the words you must use when addressing the Emperor. Japanese has different levels of respect language—such as when addressing older people or superiors. The level used for the Emperor is the most respectful of all. When the Emperor dies, two Chinese characters are written; they cannot be used to describe the death of anyone else. Among my non-Japanese colleagues at Reuters was a Canadian lady married to a Japanese man. She had excellent fluency, including command of this "imperial language" and was good mannered. She won the approval of the stony-faced IHA officials to attend the annual news conference. We, her colleagues, were full of admiration.

The most famous Irish person in Japan is Patrick Lafcadio Hearn, who lived in the country from 1890 until his death in 1904. He married a Japanese woman, and the couple had four children. He became a Japanese citizen and took the name Yakumo Koizumi. His wife was a native of Matsue in western Japan. In 1934, the city opened a memorial museum in his honour as well as his former residence; they have become two of the city's most popular tourist attractions. In the summer of 2016, the museum was re-opened after renovation and expansion. A Japanese garden in Tramore, County Waterford, is named after him, as is a cultural centre at the University of Durham. Hearn owes his fame to his writings as a journalist and author. In 1894, he published *Glimpses of Unfamiliar Japan*, a book which offered people in the West a precious view of a country and culture they knew almost nothing about. He went on to write eleven more books on Japan and became Professor of English Literature at the Imperial University of Tokyo. His last book, *Japan, An Attempt at Interpretation*, was published posthumously in 1905. All his books contained a theme of regret for the loss of customs and practices—the price for the country's relentless modernisation. Many Japanese admire this, especially coming from a foreigner. Between 1891 and 1894, he taught at a secondary school, whose principal was Kano Jigoro, the founder of Judo. Both the man and the martial art he invented profoundly influenced Hearn—another reason for Japanese to admire him. In 1987, the Irish embassy in Tokyo opened a special library devoted to books by and about him.

Hearn was born in June 1850, son of Charles Bush Hearn, from County Offaly, a surgeon in the British army, and an illiterate Greek mother. His father was stationed in Greece. The young man grew up in Ireland, a Catholic school in France and London. In 1869, he emigrated to the United States and became a reporter, magazine editor and translator. He was sent to Japan in 1890 on commission as a newspaper correspondent. After a stressful and nomadic life, he found there a home and his greatest inspiration.

Bon Koizumi, his great-grandson, is director of the memorial museum in Matsue. This is what he wrote about his famous ancestor: "Hearn was not bound by the prejudice of Western centrism. He had great insight into the essence of Meiji-era Japan and made proposals for Japan's future. 'Symbiosis with nature', 'education of the imagination', 'accepting nature as it is', 'national character and natural disasters' and 'the truth in tales of the supernatural' ... these are all themes which are relevant today. I hope that, through the museum, you are able to understand the many facets of Hearn and trace the path that led to his open mind."

As Ireland became a "Celtic Tiger", so did trade and investment links grow with Japan which has one of the world's largest economies and a consumer market of more than 120 million people. They are meticulous and demanding consumers and access to the market has not always been easy. But the path for Irish, and other EU, companies into Japan became significantly smoother after Tokyo and Brussels signed the EU-Japan Economic Partnership Agreement which came into force on February 1, 2019 and created the largest open trade zone in the world. By 2020, Japan was Ireland's 11th largest trading partner and fourth biggest outside the EU.

A symbol of Dublin's optimism in the future was "Ireland House" in central Tokyo, the biggest single investment on a building ever by the Department of Foreign Affairs, costing 23 million euros. The building it to house the embassy and ambassador's residence, office for various Irish government agencies, seminar facilities and an exhibition area.

"The vision for this new 'Ireland House' is to provide an exceptional platform for Ireland to develop an increased level of ambition and engagement in Japan in future years," the Irish government said. "In addition, the new building will help to raise Ireland's profile in Japan and showcase its arts, cultural heritage and business through excellence in design, and the construction of a landmark building."

If Lafcadio Hearn could visit Ireland House, he would surely be pleased to see it.

Sir Robert Hart, head of the Chinese Imperial Maritime Customs.

13

Is There Rice in the Congee?

In 2006, my wife and I moved back to Hong Kong. It is her home and where her family live. It has also been generous with visas to foreigners. Once they have stayed seven consecutive years, they can obtain an identity card that allows them to stay permanently. This gives them access to an excellent public health system that is low cost and heavily subsidised by the government. Since we moved here, I have devoted myself to writing books.

Louise divides books into two categories—'無米粥' and '有米粥' (*wu mi zhou, you mi zhou*), 'congee without rice' or 'congee with rice'. Congee is the porridge Cantonese like to eat, especially for breakfast. It is made by boiling water and adding whatever ingredients you have—rice, vegetables, dried fruit, meat and flavourings. Expensive congee contains all of these; but, if you buy the cheapest one, it contains few of them, or maybe none at all. So 'congee without rice' has come to mean a wasteful project, something that earns no income. It is a good description of many of the books written by many people, including me; royalties are welcome, but a pittance compared to the time, energy and money spent on the writing.

Fortunately, I started my writing career with a congee full of rice and many slices of meat and vegetables.

The book was commissioned by the Taiwan Buddhist Tzu Chi Foundation, the biggest NGO in the Chinese-speaking world. A company director, a member of the Foundation, gave a generous writing fee, plus the costs of travel and hotels, to Taiwan, South Africa, Indonesia and California. Since then, I have had eleven books published. Two were "congee with rice" – modest commissions, one from the Bangladesh Consulate-General in Hong Kong for a short book about investing in his country. The other nine were "congee without rice" – no payment. In addition, I wrote two books commissioned by wealthy Hong Kong families; both paid a monthly fee. But, in the end, they decided not to publish the book, for reasons they did not make clear. So you get the money, but no book. Other authors who write such books tell me that this is a common outcome. Rich families and large companies and institutions commission a book about themselves; but members with strong personalities hold different views as to what it should contain. Such differences of opinion become so fierce that they cannot agree on the final text – and, in the end, publish nothing.

My second book was definitely "rice without congee" – a biography of Grandfather entitled was *Frederick, the Life of My Missionary Grandfather in Manchuria* – but it had some surprises in store for me. Every year since then, the book has sparked an event somewhere in the world, in China or abroad. Once published, it took on a life of its own, beyond our control.

To collect material, Louise and I made two visits to Belfast and the Union Theological College, where the Presbyterian Church trains its ministers. Its Gamble Library has over 63,000 books and comprehensive material on the mission to Manchuria to which Grandfather belonged. We photocopied articles he wrote from China and those written about him; they were the basis of the book. Grandfather himself wrote three books about his service in China. Also very helpful were the Reverend Jack Weir: Reverend John Dunlop: and Reverend Dr Laurence Kirkpatrick, then Professor of Church History at the college, who wrote two excellent books on the church and the mission in Manchuria. In addition, Declan Kelleher, Ireland's ambassador to China, encouraged me to apply for funding from the Department of Foreign Affairs (DoFA); it graciously provided a grant in November 2010.

In Hong Kong, we were blessed to find Anne Lee, deputy chief editor of Joint Publishing (JP), a major publisher. She was brave enough to sign a first contract with an author she did not know. Declan made another critical intervention. In July 2012, he attended the Hong Kong Book Fair, the biggest event of the year for the city's publishing industry; it attracts one million visitors. At that time, we had an English but no Chinese version. Anne Lee was hesitating; she feared demand for a Chinese edition would be too low. I introduced Declan and asked him to say a few words. An Irishman and an ambassador, he did not disappoint. He spoke eloquently for ten minutes; she was moved—and agreed to a Chinese version. It came out in November 2012, in traditional characters, for the Hong Kong, Macau, Taiwan and overseas Chinese markets. In August 2013, the Beijing branch of JP published another in simplified characters, for the mainland market.

In 2013, we launched the book at the Union Theological College in Belfast, where Grandfather studied. It was an unforgettable event. In attendance were the Moderator of the Church, other ministers and relatives of missionaries who had also served in Manchuria. Geoffrey Keating from the DoFA, whom I had known as Consul-General in Shanghai, made the journey specially from Dublin to attend; he left the office after work and took a bus to Belfast. We were very touched. As often at such events, the speaker learnt more from the participants than he told them. They had a detailed knowledge of the mission in Manchuria, even though it had finished sixty years before. If Grandfather had been sitting in the room, I think, he would have been happy to see his memory honoured in this way. The DoFA was most supportive. It bought 180 copies and distributed them to people of standing in Ireland, including Northern Ireland First Minister Peter Robinson and Deputy First Minister Martin McGuiness. When the two came to Hong Kong in November 2012 on an investment mission, I met them at a reception. I suggested that they put the book on the school curriculum – the story of a man who treated everyone equally and did something significant with his life; he was a model for the young people of Northern Ireland. By the time I arrived, however, the reception had been running for more than an hour and many of the bottles were empty. So I think the First Minister did not hear a word of what I said. But Mr McGuiness did not drink, and he heard me out and nodded with a smile.

On June 28, 2013, the DoFA graciously organised a presentation of the book at Iveagh House, its Dublin headquarters. It was attended by more than fifty people, including officials from the Chinese embassy. In my remarks, I thanked the department for arranging the event.

"I would also like to say that, wherever I have worked in Asia, in Beijing, Shanghai, Hong Kong or Tokyo, the members of the department have been most courteous and friendly. They have invited me to meet leading members of the government and the academic and business communities. Without your support, Grandfather's book would never have seen the light of day."

In March 2013, we made a presentation at a Beijing bookshop attended both by Declan Kelleher and Ruairi Quinn, Minister for Education and Skills. Both made brief remarks, which made a deep impression on the audience. This is what I said: "What all this generous support adds up to is that publishers, journalists, academics and the general reader understand that this book is not simply a person writing about a grandfather but that his work and those of the other Presbyterian missionaries in Manchuria had a wider historical and moral significance."

These two talks were part of a global roadshow to promote the book. We have done presentations in Leicester, Hong Kong, Tokyo and Taipei and many interviews to the media, in English, Chinese and Japanese. We have sent copies to people all over the world, including the Archbishop of Canterbury in London and ministers, academics and interested parties in the United States, Canada, Japan, South Korea and Taiwan. The Presbyterian Church in Taiwan was set up at the same time as the one in Manchuria, and Korea; it has deep historical roots. Talk venues have included theological colleges in Hong Kong, where Christian churches are flourishing. As of 2019, there were 1.2 million Christians, 16 per cent of the total population; 800,000 are Protestant and 400,000 Catholic. The churches play a key role in providing health, education and social welfare. Hong Kong has become the global evangelisation centre for China.

To our pleasant surprise, Joint Publishing in Beijing produced a version in simplified Chinese, so we were able to promote it in mainland China. This was not a given. The government controls tightly religious activities, especially Christianity, as well as contact between Chinese believers and foreigners. Over the last twenty years, the official designation of missionaries like Grandfather has improved, from being part of the "colonial" effort to subdue China to a more nuanced view that they made a contribution in education, health and other sectors. So we were able to give public talks in Chinese at bookshops in Guangzhou, Zhuhai and Shantou. The one in Shantou, at its university, attracted about 100 people, in a lecture hall. The campus is some distance from the city centre; there was not much to do in the evening. So a talk by a Big-Nose was better than watching television. We invited the pastor from the city's Protestant church to attend, and he came. We asked him to come to the stage and say a few words – he was the real descendant of Grandfather in Shantou, not me. But he declined – experience had taught him to keep a low profile.

Once we had the simplified Chinese version, we wanted to take it to Faku and present copies to the ministers and congregation there. This was not so simple. Faku is an "open" place, which means that foreigners are allowed to visit. But few do because it has no famous historical sites or special products that people wish to buy. Since religion is a sensitive issue, town officials want to monitor any contact between an outsider and local church members. Preferring not to meet the officials, we gave no prior notice of our arrival. We took a taxi from the provincial capital of Shenyang, about an hour on an expressway, and arrived in mid-morning. Fortunately, the minister was in the church at the time, together with members of her congregation. They were delighted with the books. One remarked: "Why do we have to learn our own history from a foreigner?" After a warm and moving lunch together, we left Faku in the afternoon. We did not see the officials – our good fortune.

In the provincial capital of Shenyang, scholars and ministers began to buy the book and take an interest in Grandfather's story. Some sent us e-mails and questions about him. Later we learnt that the Faku church, built in 1907, was under threat from a nearby real estate project called Caesar's Palace. The developers wanted to demolish the building to open up more land for their project. But they did not succeed, for two reasons. One was lobbying by those scholars who argued that the town should preserve the structure as part of its history. The other was that, as in other cities, many of the units in Caesar's Palace went unsold, so there was in the end no need to build new ones.

The next unexpected development was Grandfather's entry into the official history of the anti-Japanese war, as a result of something he did in the spring of 1932. At that time a British peer named Lord Lytton led a commission to Manchuria; it was appointed by the League of Nations to judge whether the new state of Manchukuo, established by Japan, reflected the will of the Manchurian people or was simply a puppet of Tokyo. The Japanese officials rolled out the red carpet for the five members of the commission; this made it impossible for them to contact Chinese people without such officials present – which prevented them from speaking honestly. So a group of eminent Chinese in Shenyang asked Grandfather to present a box of documents to Lord Lytton; as a foreigner, he could have a private meeting with him, which they could not. Grandfather agreed at once. He arranged a dinner in the house of a missionary in Shenyang; it was a small house and the dining room cramped. So, citing the lack of space, he asked the Japanese officials to wait outside during the meal. This gave him the opportunity to give the documents to Lord Lytton without the knowledge of the Japanese. They played an important role in the commission's report that was published on October 2, 1932. It found that Manchukuo could not have been established without the presence of Japanese troops and was not the result of a genuine independence movement. In February 1933, the Japanese representative walked out of the League of Nations in protest; it was a first step toward World War Two. This collection of documents is now in the Library and Archives of the United Nations in Geneva.

This action by Grandfather, described in two pages in the book, suddenly became the subject of newspaper and academic articles in China, as part of the "Anti-Japanese Struggle". A crew from Tianjin Television came to south China to interview me. We met in a hotel in Guangzhou. The producer rented a room; she shot me playing the role of Grandfather as he wrote the letter to Lord Lytton asking for a meeting. She turned off the lights in the room, except for a table lamp which showed me writing it. I learnt that the entire programme was about Grandfather's passing the documents to Lord Lytton and nothing else. I thanked her for making the programme but added: "I wonder if you could make a second programme about his work for the people of Faku in health, education and religion."

She smiled. "Of course we cannot make such a programme!" she replied. "With your knowledge of China, I am surprised that you ask such a stupid question."

What she meant that the role of foreigners could only be presented as part of an official narrative on the "Anti-Japanese Patriotic War" and not for anything else. Subsequently, we have received more inquiries about this event. In 2020, a Shenyang publishing house brought out a children's book about it and sent me a copy. To each caller, I stressed that the bravery of Grandfather was modest compared to that of the Chinese who prepared the documents. If they had been caught, they would have been arrested and interrogated by the Japanese and probably tortured if they did not co-operate. By comparison, the worst case outcome for Grandfather would have been expulsion from Manchuria, with no physical injury.

Grandfather's next surprise for us came in the summer of 2012. I was in the house of a relative in London, packing for the flight back to Hong Kong the next day. Across the other side of the world, an Irish friend in Beijing sent me an e-mail: "Buy *The Irish Times* today and read page eight." I went to a nearby grocery; fortunately, it had one copy of the paper left, which I bought. The article on page eight said that a medal which Grandfather received in 1919 from the Chinese government for his service to

Chinese labourers in France in World War One would be sold at auction the next week at a hotel in Hong Kong. Louise said that this was Grandfather giving us the chance to buy the piece; if we did not, we would lose it forever. The timing was perfect – one day of flying and one day of recuperating, and we were at the Holiday Inn Golden Mile in Hong Kong. I asked the auctioneer, a British man, the identity of the person selling the medal. "Cannot tell you," he said. "That is confidential."

I told him that I suspected it was a distant cousin of mine who suddenly needed money, for a house renovation or his child's school fees; who else would have been able to obtain the medal? Despite my best charm, the auctioneer would give no clues. The auction room was crowded, mainly with mainland Chinese who had come to buy the main items in the auction – coins from China's early Republican period, from 1911 to 1930. For them, money was no object – prices of US$30,000 or more for the coins. After an hour, the medal came on the auction block. Its name was "Order of the Striped Tiger," Fifth Class, in silver-gilt and enamels, 60 mm, in its original lacquer box. Fortunately, the piece was of no interest to the wealthy bidders in the room. There was only one other bidder, by telephone. The price went quickly from US$1,000, each time by US$500, up to US$4,500 by our competitor. What to do? Grandfather would not have wanted us to pay so much – and the piece was brass, not gold or silver. There were seconds to decide; I was hesitating. Louise put up her hand, at US$5,000 – and there was no other bid. So, after paying a large commission in addition, we found ourselves in possession of the medal. As always, Louise was correct to buy the piece. If we had not, it would have disappeared without trace. After keeping it in a box in our small apartment for some months, we decided to donate it to the Presbyterian Church in Belfast; that is where it belongs.

Grandfather's most recent appearance was in an exhibition "Irish Educators Abroad" by the EPIC Irish Emigration Museum in Custom House Quay in Dublin in the summer of 2019. The museum graciously invited us to give a presentation, which we did on August 22. We had an excellent audience that included diplomats, academics, Chinese Christians and a minister from a nearby Presbyterian church. What is certain is that Grandfather has not finished with us yet. He has more surprises in store for us, in China and abroad. His book, in simplified characters, is on sale on e-commerce websites in China. This is what would please him most, I think; the people of mainland China can read about what he and the other missionaries did for them. For this Chinese version, we must thank Anne Lee of Joint Publishing and Declan's critical intervention at the Book Fair in July 2012.

It was an e-mail from Declan that triggered another book about an Irishman in China—also "congee without rice". His e-mail contained a photograph of a street sign in central Beijing—"Rue de Hart". After 1949, the new government renamed the streets of China's cities that bore the names of foreigners. It was part of its effort to rid the country of foreign influence. But, 60 years later, this sign had somehow survived, next to the new post-1949 Chinese name. Sir Robert Hart was Inspector-General of the China's Imperial Maritime Customs Service (IMCS) from 1863 until his death in 1911. It was the highest post in the Chinese government ever held by a foreigner, and for the longest period. No non-Chinese will have such a career in the future. "How about a biography of Sir Robert?" Declan said. He often spoke about Sir Robert and his influence on him and his work in China.

A little research showed what a good idea it was. Sir Robert's life was similar to that of Grandfather. Brought up in a religious family in the north of Ireland, he spent all his working life in China and only returned home at the age of 73, at the urging of his wife and family. Grandfather would have stayed all his life in Faku too; but, in December 1941, he was detained by the Japanese after the attack on Pearl Harbour; he was expelled from China in the summer of 1942. After the war, he would have liked to return, but was too old. The two men were similar in character: studious, disciplined, moral and investing heavily in the study of written and spoken Mandarin. They had a range and depth of Chinese friends rare among foreigners of their generation. Both were "good" foreigners; they contributed greatly to their adopted country. They make us proud to speak of them with Chinese people. The same cannot be said of many foreigners who were there between 1850 and 1945, when it was a semi-colonial country. While Grandfather served God and the people of Manchuria, Sir Robert served the Chinese government for 48 years; he represented it in many negotiations with foreign nations – much to the surprise of officials of these countries who saw a Big-nose across the table. His department contributed a substantial part of the government's revenue, up to one third in some years. This money paid for armaments and machinery factories, shipyards and vessels that became China's modern navy. He set up a fleet of patrol vessels and lighthouses along China's coast and, in 1896, established its first postal service. So it was an easy decision to propose a biography. Anne Lee of Joint Publishing was happy to accept it, with the title *Ireland's Imperial Mandarin* with and versions in English and Chinese

Writing the biography was not difficult. Between 1854 and 1907, Sir Robert wrote detailed letters and journals. We owe their survival to Leslie Sandercock, one of his assistants. He heroically rescued 70 volumes of them from his house in Beijing – in Rue de Hart – as the Boxers were burning it down in June 1900. The rest of the house was destroyed. The journals are now in the archives of Queens University, Belfast. What makes the journals so valuable for a biographer is that Sir Robert did not write them for publication but for himself and his closest friend, the IMCS representative in London. So we find a frankness and honesty he could not use in official documents for his superiors in the Qing government. This is especially the case regarding his greatest secret—his Chinese sweetheart, Miss Ayaou, and the three children she had with him. To become Inspector-General, he decided that he had to leave her. He married an Irish lady of similar class to himself; they also had three children. The rules of upper class society at that time, in China as in the West, would not have allowed a mixed marriage, especially to the daughter of a boatman in Ningbo, which Miss Ayaou was. When Sir Robert became Inspector-General in 1863, he paid her the substantial sum of 3,000 dollars, on condition that he took their three children away to be brought up and educated in Britain. He did not want them to remain in China, where his Irish wife or other people could find them. In a life of remarkable moral probity, this was the unkindest thing he did, to take the three away from their mother and have them raised in an alien place. To keep the secret, he rarely wrote in later life about Miss Ayaou and the children, except in letters to his London friend to ask about the money to support them and their education. As far as we know, Sir Robert succeeded—his wife and her three children never learnt of this secret family. But he could never be sure. In later life, Lady Hart lived in London, in Cadogan Square, Kensington, one of the city's most expensive areas. The three children also lived in London but in a more downmarket district—the two families inhabited different universes and had no reason to meet.

To fill this hole in our narrative, we turned to a novel written by a Chinese historian, Zhao Changtian, *An Irishman in China*. Like us, Zhao was fascinated by Hart's secret romance; if he could not write it as history, then he would write it as a novel.

In a blog published in February 2010, he said that he spent three years on the book and read 15 million words of source material. "In China, Hart was a special and important person, with streets named after him in Shanghai and Beijing."

When I gave talks on the book, the first question from the audience was not about the decline of the Qing dynasty or the finances of the Customs Service, but always about Hart's double life. In Zhao's account, the beautiful Miss Ayaou was the love of Hart's life. From a modest family, she was vivacious and free of the social and sexual constraints of women – Chinese and Western – from the middle and upper classes. Shy and self-controlled, Hart could suddenly relax and be himself. For professional expatriates like him, a paid Chinese mistress for a limited period was the norm; then they paid off the mistress and married a suitable partner, who often had to be brought from the home country. What made Hart different was the length and intensity of his relationship with Miss Ayaou. She also played a critical role in improving his knowledge of Mandarin and Chinese society and customs; it was this that enabled him to persuade high officials of the court in Beijing to hire him and employ him for more than forty years. He paid a heavy personal price for his choice. Lady Hart lived in Beijing for only fourteen years before she took their three children back to Britain. This was not surprising. China's capital was a dusty, backward city with few of the comforts she had enjoyed in Ireland and very little for an expatriate woman to do. Had they lived in Shanghai, Tianjin, Guangzhou or other foreign concession cities, it would have been different. The largest, Shanghai, had a big foreign community, with department stores, banks, restaurants, bars, dance halls, a racecourse and many other conveniences of a modern city. Beijing only suited foreigners who, like Sir Robert, were absorbed in their work. After his wife left, he spent the last 26 years of his life alone in his large house in the Rue de Hart, with his servants, violin, Latin books, brass band, amateur theatricals and busy social life. If Miss Ayaou had been Lady Hart, he would have had a happier life.

In Faku today, you can see the legacy of Grandfather—his house and the church and schools he built. But this is not the case for Sir Robert. We went to the Rue de Hart, a narrow street of grey brick buildings in the Dongcheng (East City) district. The buildings belong to state institutions and the gates are locked. In Sir Robert's day, it was the Foreign Legation quarter. The best we could do was the Chinese Customs Museum, next to the national headquarters of the Customs. It contains photographs of Sir Robert and the ICMS. Its judgement of him is different to the one presented by western historians: while he worked for the Qing government, Sir Robert was primarily serving the interests of foreign powers, especially the British, it said. The family line died out in October 1970, with the death of a grandson, also called Robert, the third baronet. He had no children. So there were no descendants to contact and share information with.

After he left Beijing in 1908, Sir Robert spent the final three years of his life in England and Ireland. While he was feted everywhere, like Grandfather, he felt out of place. He had spent so long in China and given so much of himself there. He was delighted to be Pro-Chancellor of his alma mater, Queen's University, from 1909 to 1911. He donated generously to the university, toward a building for its Student Union and Better Equipment Fund. In the autumn of 1908, he gave speeches in Belfast and Dublin. The best one was in Lisburn, his native place, on November 30. "You are Irishmen and I am afraid that the Blarney Stone has to some extent affected this part of the county. I have been suffering from the same complaint ever since my return from China. It is more than my modest nature as an

Irishman can bear." He gave the credit for his achievements at the ICMS to Chinese and foreigners with whom he worked. "I could not claim to be much more than the grease which helped to make the wheel revolve more easily." He praised many aspects of Chinese society, especially Confucian ethics and the merit-based exam system for the civil service. In the 1860s, he said, he asked the Prime Minister of China about the many difficulties the country faced. The response: "I can give you a prescription for preventing difficulties. Go back to your own country and mind your own business, and leave us alone to mind ours."

Our promotion efforts for Sir Robert's book were less ambitious than those for Grandfather. We sent a copy to President Michael Higgins and did presentations at the Hong Kong and Taipei Book Fairs and at other venues in Shanghai, Hong Kong, Macau and London. We also did many interviews with the media.

In August 2014, the Department of Foreign Affairs and Trade opened the first Consulate-General in Hong Kong, with Peter Ryan as Consul-General. He rented an office on the 20th floor of the Bank of East Asia building in Des Voeux Road, an excellent location a few minutes from the Central subway station in downtown. The official opening came on September 18 2015, with Minister for Jobs, Enterprise and Innovation, Richard Bruton TD as guest of honour.

The consulate joined several Irish organisations—Irish Chambers of Commerce in both Hong Kong and Macau, the St Patrick's Society in Hong Kong, the Irish International Education Centre, the Celtic Connections Choir and the Hong Kong Gaelic Athletic Association, which was founded in 1995. There are also four schools of Irish dance: Conradh na Gaelige: Emerald Fund, Irish Funds, the Ireland Funds of China: the Irish Working Holiday Union: and the Irish Whiskey Society of Hong Kong & Macau.

Peter had plenty to work with – 5,000 citizens and 6,000 local graduates from Irish universities. Most of the 5,000 were professionals, like bankers, accountants, teachers, priests and in IT and fintech; some had lived in the city for decades. He quickly established the Irish presence. He organised the first St Patrick's Parade along the waterfront on the north shore of Hong Kong harbour to Tamar Park in front of the main government building. A tram painted green drove the length of the city; on March 17, major buildings were bathed in green. In 2020, Ireland exported to Hong Kong goods worth US$798 million, mainly meat, dairy products, seafood and alcoholic drinks.

I was one of many beneficiaries of Peter's hard work – he organised events to promote my books. The advantage was that people who would not come to an event I put on would attend one arranged by a Consul-General. So it was with one at the consulate on a book entitled *Israel & China: from the Tang Dynasty to Silicon Wadi*. Thanks to him, both the Israeli consul-general and a prominent Rabbi attended. Peter ordered kosher food, which was extremely thoughtful. As we waited for Peter's speech, we were unsure what the Irish 'angle' would be; he did not disappoint. He spoke of Robert Briscoe, the first Jewish Lord Mayor of Dublin, in 1956, and a TD in the Fianna Fail party in the Oireachtas (Parliament) from 1927 to 1965. His son Ben also served as Lord Mayor from 1988-89. "So Dublin had a Jewish mayor before New York," said Peter. The first Jewish mayor of that city was Abraham Beame, who held the post from 1974 to 1977 Robert Briscoe was Lord Mayor of Dublin in 1956, 18 years before Beame was Mayor of NY. Even better, the sixth president of Israel, Chaim Herzog, was Irish. He was born in Belfast in 1918, son of Ireland's Chief Rabbi, and grew up mainly in Dublin. He emigrated to Palestine in 1935; after a distinguished military career, he served as president from 1983 to 1993. The 11th president, elected in June 2021, is Isaac Herzog, son of Chaim. As Peter was speaking, I watched the expressions of the rabbi and the Consul-General; both were enchanted – this story was news to them. This guaranteed their full attention for the book presentation; and I have remained friends with the two ever since. Is this not the mission of a diplomat, to bring people together?

A Jewish friend in Hong Kong later told me of another important page in relations between Ireland and the Jewish people – their generosity during the Great Famine. In March 1847, two synagogues in New York collected nearly US$2,000 for those suffering from hunger in Ireland. The same year, in London, Lionel de Rothschild and friends set up the British Association for the Relief of Distress in Ireland and the Highlands of Scotland; it raised 600,000 pounds from 15,000 individuals around the world. De Rothschild oversaw the opening of schools and distribution centres to provide food across Ireland. This was the biggest single aid donation to the country during the Famine. By comparison, U.S. President James Polk gave US$50 and Queen Victoria 2,000 pounds.

One of Peter's biggest achievements was to persuade Cathay Pacific to launch a direct flight from Hong Kong to Dublin; it was the first direct flight between the capital and a city in Asia. At four times a week, it began service on June 2, 2018. The target was not only Hong Kong people but also mainlanders; 70,000 of them visited Ireland in 2017. "People here want 'experienced-based travel," said Robert Agnew, chairman of the European Chamber of Commerce and one author of a survey of the Hong Kong market for Tourism Ireland. "They like 'clean and green'. We need a strong presence on Facebook and WeChat. Racing holidays are full of potential. 3,000 Hong Kong people own or part-own racehorses. Of the horses here, ten per cent are Irish." Unfortunately, in November 2019, Cathay suspended for four months the new service because of insufficient capacity. With the Covid-19 pandemic, the suspension became long-term.

Through Peter's work and connections, I began to see more clearly the remarkable Irish history in Hong Kong. Of the 28 governors before the handover in 1997, nine were Irish. They were joined by thousands of soldiers, policemen, judges, doctors, teachers, priests, nuns, architects, accountants, jockeys, entrepreneurs and people in other walks of life. I described some of them in Chapter Ten, including Sister Mary Aquinas and her lifetime battle with tuberculosis. The ones who impressed me most were the religious; they devoted their lives to serving Hong Kong people in education, health, pastoral care and religion, like Grandfather in Manchuria. When the complex history of colonialism is written, their contribution will be a large entry into the positive column. One measure of this is the vibrant alumni associations of the schools they ran. These former students, living here as well as in cities around the world to which Hong Kong people have emigrated, eagerly support their schools with funds and reunions and warmly welcome their former teachers. This reflects their deep gratitude for how the schools transformed their lives – providing a modern education in English to children often of refugee families with little money; it enabled them to become business people and professionals, earn good salaries and, if they wished, make a comfortable life in a foreign country.

During my second stay in Hong Kong, I had the good fortune to meet several of these priests, in their 70s and 80s. Over the last 30 years, the number of vocations in Ireland, as in other countries in Western Europe, has dropped dramatically. No young priests have come, a matter of great regret for them but something they have learnt to live with. The missing Irish priests and nuns have been replaced with ones from China, Hong Kong, Philippines, India, South Korea and other countries. I met two of the elderly

Jesuits, Father Harold Naylor and Father Alfred Deignan. I met Father Naylor in Wah Yan College in Kowloon, in the room where he had lived for forty years. The floor was home to him and his fellow priests. We talked in the reception and dining room on the same floor. What a good place to grow old, I thought to myself. Everyone in the school—teachers, staff and students—knew who he was. In 1951, he joined the Society of Jesus in Ireland and came to Hong Kong in 1960. He worked at Wah Yan College from 1967 to 2016; in 1968, with two others, he co-founded the first conservation group in Hong Kong. For 25 years, he operated a club for poor children. He showed me the memorial plaque laid in his honour in the school garden. After his death on October 4, 2018, aged 87, his remains were donated, as he wished, to Hong Kong University for medical studies.

Father Deignan arrived here even earlier, in 1953. He also served as a teacher and principal of the Wah Yan colleges in Hong Kong and Kowloon. Between 1970 and 1978, he was warden of Ricci Hall, a university residence run by the Jesuits; it was there I met him, graceful and dignified. He passed away on December 11, 2018, aged 91. In his honour, on June 22, 2022, the Macau Ricci Institute and the Wofoo Social Enterprises launched the Deignan Award for Responsible Entrepreneurship, to encourage ethical practices in business and help them create sustainable business models guided by justice, solidarity and responsibility. They will pick one Small & Medium Enterprise each in Hong Kong and Macao, and later in the Greater Bay Area. Dr Stephan Rothlin, also a Jesuit, is Director of the Macau Ricci Institute and chief executive of Rothlin International Management, with offices in Hong Kong and Beijing. He has been involved in the research and promotion of business ethics in China, Hong Kong and Macao for more than 20 years. "I had the chance to work with Father Deignan over many years on different projects of business ethics. The example of this deeply compassionate educator with a passion of sharing key values of integrity, compassion and honesty left a decisive mark in various circles of society. In these times of crisis, the Deignan Award would be a very inspiring way to demonstrate the positive impact of sound values which could open a light and make a difference in a very demanding and competitive market place," he said.

In August 2018, Peter Ryan was succeeded as Consul-General by David Costello. He decided to commission a book on the Irish of Hong Kong and asked me to help him write it. What started as a modest project grew into two thick volumes. We were astonished by the depth and diversity of the Irish presence here. God and the pandemic permitting, we hope that the book will be published one day.

During the 2021 Tokyo Olympics, a 23-year-old woman with a glowing smile became the most famous Irish person on Hong Kong. Swimmer Siobhán Bernadette Haughey won two silver medals in the 100-metre and 200-metre freestyle events. She was the first Hong Kong athlete to win two Olympic medals. It was a remarkable achievement. The Chinese-language newspapers call her "Little Beautiful Mermaid" (小美魚人). She chose to swim for Hong Kong rather than Ireland, because she was born and grew up there. She delighted the Hong Kong media and public by speaking fluent Cantonese, as well as Mandarin and English. Few foreigners in Hong Kong speak Cantonese so well, even those who have lived in the city many years. Her ease of manner with all kinds of people greatly impressed the public. Her father's uncle is Charles Haughey, Taoiseach on three separate occasions totalling seven years between 1979 and 1992.

The daughter of Irish accountant Darach Haughey and his wife Canjo. Siobhán was born on 31 October, 1997 and grew up in Happy Valley. Her Chinese name is Ho Si-pui (何詩蓓). She and elder sister Aisling first got their feet wet in a pool in their building. When she was four, the two girls were sent to the South China Athletic Association (SCAA) in Causeway Bay. "I did not enjoy it at all," she recalled. "It was very boring, just swimming up and down the pool, and I would cry every time I went." Fortunately, Canjo was a 'tiger mother' who would not take no for an answer. "After a while, I saw those swimming lessons as a chance to see my friends, rather than to learn how to swim," Siobhán said. "At that age, when you have friends with you, everything seems more enjoyable." Despite a heavy training schedule, she also excelled at secondary school, scoring a total of 35 points from seven subjects in the Hong Kong Diploma of Secondary Education. She scored four out of five in Chinese, known as "the paper of death" (死亡之科)—nearly half the candidates in Hong Kong fail each year.

Her former coach Michael Fasching said: "She had the perfect build to be a swimmer and was mentally strong. Her physical attributes combined with tremendous discipline. There were not many other athletes who were as disciplined and focused as she was." Elder sister Aisling chose to settle in Darach's hometown of Dublin; she is now a physiotherapist. Siobhán chose to study at the University of Michigan in the United States and graduated in 2019 with a bachelor's degree in psychology.

Hazel Chu, mayor of Dublin.

14

Chinese in Ireland

In much of this book, we have described the contribution of Irish people to other places, England, Scotland, China, Hong Kong and Japan. This chapter looks at the Chinese going the other way. They began in restaurants but have now risen to political office, and positions in banks, factories, law firms, computer laboratories and hospitals. Let us start with the most prominent one.

On June 29, 2020 Hazel Chu, daughter of two Hong Kong immigrants, became the 352nd Lord Mayor of Dublin. She was the first ethnic Chinese to hold office in the Republic, and the first to be mayor of a major European capital. It was a milestone in the history of Chinese migration to Ireland. For centuries a country of emigration, Ireland has now become open-minded and wealthy enough to attract large numbers of foreigners.

In the census of April 2016, 11.6 per cent of the population were non-Irish nationals. It put the number of Chinese at 9,575; Asians as a whole accounted for 2.1 per cent of the population. Chinese go to Ireland for same reasons that Irish people went to China. It offers them jobs, salaries, opportunities and space and freedom they cannot find at home.

When Sir Robert and Grandfather went to live in China, it was the "sick man of Asia", unable and unwilling to follow the example of Japan and modernise in order to combat the colonial powers. But peace and prosperity, for 70 years in Hong Kong and 40 years in the mainland, have created an economic boom unprecedented in China's history. Millions of Chinese are now highly educated, well qualified and with the money and means to emigrate to other countries.

It was the restaurant business that brought the parents of Hazel Chu – and the vast majority of Chinese to Ireland – during the 1970s. Chu's parents emigrated separately from Hong Kong and went to work in the same restaurant off O'Connell Street in central Dublin, where they met. Her mother Stella came from a poor family in Hong Kong, where she sold flowers in a market after school to earn money. After moving to Dublin, she worked day and night washing dishes in the restaurant. In her acceptance speech, Chu said that her mother "worked endlessly to give us a future she never had". The family lived in Firhouse and Celbridge, suburbs of Dublin. The parents worked so much that they had to place their daughter in a boarding school. Hazel described Stella as a 'tiger mother' never satisfied with her grades. After her parents divorced, Stella opened four restaurants; her father returned to his home village to open a café there.

A gifted student, Chu studied history and politics at University College, Dublin (UCD), where she ran debating competitions and the Philosophy Society. Then she completed a legal diploma and barrister-at-law degree at King's Inn. She was the first Irish-born of Chinese descent to be called to the Irish bar. But she did not practice as a barrister because she urgently needed money to pay back the tuition fees. After being called to the Bar in 2007, she worked in Sydney, Hong Kong and Guilin, China and New York. She worked as an artist and production manager for Electric Picnic, a music festival: a fund-raising manager for a charity: a marketing consultant in New York for Bord Bia, the Irish Food Board: advisory posts in government institutions: and six years as head of communications for Diageo Ireland. Diageo is one of the world's largest sellers of wines and spirits.

"My mother would describe me as a grafter and jack of all trades, but master of none!" she said.

In 2014, she became involved in politics when managing a local election in a Dublin district for her partner Patrick Costello. She organised campaigning on social media, the news media and door-to-door canvassing. He came top in the polls. This success prompted her to run for election herself. Patrick is now a TD for the Green Party. They married in June 2021 and have one daughter. Hazel joined the Green Party in 2016. In November 2019, the party's members elected her as chairperson. She held the post of Lord Mayor for one year until June 2021.

In the North, the earliest arrivals also went into the restaurant business. China's new government after 1949 closed the country to the outside world; it was virtually impossible to leave. But residents of Hong Kong were free to migrate. Foreign governments, like those of Ireland and Britain, were willing to give visas to restaurant chefs and their staff because they had skills which local people did not possess.

For the migrants, working in a restaurant was convenient because it did not require knowledge of English or additional training; it meant living in a Chinese environment and out of sight of immigration officials. It was lucrative – owners employ members of their family, clan or village, keeping wages low; it is a cash business, making it possible to minimise – or sometimes eliminate – payment of taxes.

When I worked in Belfast in the 1970s, I often went to Chinese restaurants in the area around Queen's University. They were among the few in the city open in the evenings; the others had closed for lack of customers and fear of paramilitary attack. I asked the owner of one why he opened after dark. "Compared to others, this district is safe. In addition, our skin colour gives us protection. We are not orange or green and so are not a target. Business is good." When I asked if he had to pay 'protection money' to one or more paramilitary group, he smiled and declined to answer. Sometimes they were asked if they were Protestant or Catholic. Their answer: "Buddhist" or "Taoist".

The work was, and is, gruelling. The restaurants were open seven days a week, leaving little time for family or leisure. While children engaged with society in school, sports and outside activities, their parents were largely prisoners of their employment—and often having to repay the money they borrowed in order to emigrate. The hard work and long hours paid off. The owners saved money and were able to made additional investments.

One Chinese bought a sturdy Presbyterian church on the corner of Donegall Pass and the Ormeau Road in Belfast and converted it into a restaurant, the "Water Margin". This is the name of a Chinese novel of the 14th century, considered one of the country's four great classical novels. This was a dramatic symbol of change—churches empty due to a fall in the number of believers and Chinese entrepreneurs having earned enough money to buy and convert them.

The rise of Hazel Chu from a child of parents who could not read or write English to a white-collar professional is the dream of every Chinese migrant. Parents work extremely hard, save money and push their children to study and pass exams. They do not want their children to have the life they had. Hazel's mother Stella was a "tiger lady", a mother who was never satisfied. But, while this title has a negative connotation—too much pressure and too little tolerance—she is a model in her community.

But not everything goes smoothly. The Achilles heel of Chinese, men and women, is not drugs or alcohol, but gambling, among themselves or at casinos and racecourses. Some of the best intentions of parents disappear down the pockets of bookies or their poker and mah-jong partners.

The second wave of Chinese immigrants into Ireland, since the 1970s, were better prepared than Hazel's parents. They came from Hong Kong, Malaysia, Taiwan and Singapore. Most came as students; after graduation, they found a job and settled down.

The third wave, since the 1990s, has also been students, from mainland China. The students were well-educated, from middle-class or wealthy families, and arrived with self-confidence and a certain fluency in English.

Many from outside mainland China attended mission schools and studied under foreign teachers, some of them Irish. So they had an acquaintance of westerners and their world, which the cook and dishwashers from rural Hong Kong did not have.

After graduating from an Irish university, they were well equipped to apply for a job, especially if they had skills in demand, like accounting, medicine, computer engineering, IT, finance and civil engineering. They had a good command of English and a network of professors, classmates and friends to help them make a life in a new country.

The funniest film about a Chinese in Ireland is "Yu Ming is Ainm Dom" (My Name is Yu Ming), a thirteen-minute comedy made in 2003 by Daniel O'Hara, mostly in the Irish language. Yu Ming is a shopworker in China bored with his life. He spins a globe and picks a country – Ireland. An atlas tells him that its official language is Gaelic; so he learns it and becomes fluent before he makes his trip.

On arrival in Dublin, he is delighted to practise what he has learnt. But no-one can understand him; they think he is talking Chinese. In a bar, he asks the barman: "*Tá mé ag lorg obair*" (I am looking for work). The barman shakes his head, not catching a word. Fortunately, there is an elderly Irish-speaker at the end of the bar; he listens in awe to the Asian speaking his language fluently. He buys him a drink and explains the misunderstanding.

Friends help Yu Ming find a job as a bartender in the Irish-speaking Gaeltacht in Connemara – a happy ending to the film.

In the 1960s, an early destination of Chinese migrants was Belfast and other cities in the North. Since it was part of Britain, it was more familiar to Hong Kong people than the Republic. I once visited the head office of a Chinese food chain in London, and on the wall was a large map of the United Kingdom, with dozens of pins in it, showing where Chinese restaurants had been set up. "When new arrivals come, we show them the map and they choose a town or city with no or few pins," said one of the staff. Another reason why Chinese chose the North was their belief it would be safer than inner city areas in Britain.

The first Chinese restaurant, the Peacock, opened in Belfast in 1962. British immigration law allowed visas to those who had arranged a job in advance. This enabled the owners to bring families and friends to work in their restaurants. Cheap property prices and the wide geographical spread of town and villages were also an attraction. By the mid-2000s, there were more than 500 Chinese restaurants in the North.

The business requires long and exhausting hours, leaving limited time for looking after their children. The staff did not have the extended family network they enjoyed at home. So some decided to send their children back to Hong Kong to be brought up by relatives. They kept a low profile, in order not to attract attention to themselves, especially after the outbreak of the Troubles in 1969.

Those working in the restaurant business saved hard, with the aim of a better life for their children. They encouraged their children to advance in their education as far as they could go.

Some have become doctors, professors, accountants, business people and entrepreneurs.

As the community settled, it set up its own institutions – the Chinese Chamber of Commerce and Chinese Welfare Association (CWA). The CWA built the Chinese Resource Centre, at a cost of 1.32 million pounds, near the Ormeau Bridge in Belfast. It opened in September 2011; with 880 square metres, it has a state-of-the-art multipurpose hall, training rooms, library, conference rooms, creche and playground. It aims to enhance diversity and develop the participation of Chinese people in all aspects of social, cultural, economic and public life in N.I.

Today there are about 10,000 Chinese in Northern Ireland, making them the second largest ethnic minority after the 30,000 Poles.

One pillar of the community in the North is the Belfast Chinese Christian Church (BCCC), on Lorne Street in Belfast. From the 1970s, Chinese students held religious meetings in the city. The number and activities grew so rapidly that they needed a home church of their own.

In November 1998, they purchased the Ulsterville Presbyterian Church in Lorne Street. It became the home of the BCCC. Today it has services on Sundays and during the week in English, Cantonese and Mandarin.

The church caters both to immigrants from Hong Kong who speak Cantonese and to those from the mainland and Taiwan, who speak Mandarin. It is a very active congregation, including Sunday school and other activities. It fosters close relations with other Protestant churches and Chinese missionary groups in Britain.

"The leadership prays that the BCCC can reach out more effectively to the Chinese in Northern Ireland," it says on its website. "But, since many local Chinese still see Christianity as a

Western religion, the task of preaching the Cross to the Chinese people will continue to be a difficult one. But we do praise God that the work continues to grow and the congregation continues to increase in numbers." Were Grandfather to visit the BCCC, I think he would be very happy; not only have Chinese accepted the Gospel, they are now considering how to spread it to the Irish and other Europeans.

During one visit there, the pastor, who was from Hong Kong, pointed to a room in the church full of children playing happily. "They will be the evangelists of the future," he told me. "They have grown up here, speak English well and understand local people and culture. You Westerners are losing your faith. These children will bring it back to you."

The chairman of the church is Dr Simon Au Dat-bun, a consultant physician at Lagan Valley Hospital in Lisburn since March 2005. He is interested in General Medicine with a special interest in Endocrinology and Diabetes. He also works at two private medical clinics, in Belfast and Hillsborough. He is a Fellow of the Royal College of Physicians in the UK, in London and Edinburgh.

Born in Hong Kong, Dr Au went to study at Queens University Belfast in 1988. He qualified as a medical doctor in 1993. He completed basic medical training in Belfast and Cardiff and also worked at the Royal Victoria, Belfast City and Craigavon Area hospitals.

The best known Chinese person in Northern Ireland is Anna Manwah Lo, the first and so far the only politician from an ethnic minority to be elected at a regional level in Northern Ireland. She was the first ethnic Chinese parliamentarian in Europe.

She was born in Hong Kong in June 1950 and grew up in a public housing estate in North Point. She moved to Northern Ireland in 1974 with her then husband, David Watson, a journalist. In her early years, she worked for the BBC and as an interpreter for the Royal Ulster Constabulary. She became a social worker. In 1999, she was awarded an MBE for her services to ethnic minorities and championing openness and equality.

She became involved with the moderate Alliance Party and was elected as a member of the Northern Ireland Assembly for Belfast South in 2007, a post she held for nine years. She was selected as the party's candidate for the N.I. constituency in the 2014 European Parliament election. She won the most votes for the party ever in a European election. But she did not stand for re-election in 2016 because of racial abuse by Ulster loyalists. Her politics were liberal and progressive.

Her two adult sons and many of her colleagues urged her to move to England for safety. She decided not to. In May 2016, she retired from politics to concentrate on charity and community work. She lives in Holywood, a comfortable suburb of Belfast. She was a former chairperson of the CWA in the North.

Is Baby Catherine Irish?

In every Chinatown in the world, you will find restaurants, fresh food markets, traditional medicine shops, supermarkets – and law offices. Many of their clients are Chinese who are illegal or have overstayed their visa. The lawyers advise them how to legalise their situation; there are many ways – marry the citizen of the country, get a work visa through a big company that will sponsor them or sign up for further years of study. The lawyers scour legislation and the media to find openings for their clients.

In the U.S, I learnt of another way Chinese become a citizen – go to a Chinese cemetery and find the tombstone of a legal citizen of the same sex, age and size as yourself. You "become" that person. You learn their personal details; then pay taxes and utility bills and acquire a car licence and social welfare documents using the name. You hope the authorities will not find out that you "died". Fake marriages were also big business in the U.S. A foreigner paid an American up to US$10,000 to go through a wedding; from there, he or she can start on the road to citizenship. I even met Americans who "married" for a living. But the Immigration Department has become well aware of this abuse. They ask detailed and intimate questions of the couple, in separate interviews, to determine if they are actually living together. What is his favourite baseball team, cereal, perfume, the colour of his underwear and favoured brand of condom? In the interview, it is easy to make a mistake, and as a result, this route has become much more hazardous.

The lawyers are constantly looking for ways to obtain citizenship. They quickly spotted an opportunity in the Nineteenth Amendment to the Irish Constitution, added in 1999. This said that anyone born on the island of Ireland was a citizen. Immediately non-nationals, including Chinese, came to Ireland to give birth to their children, who would thereby acquire a passport valid across the EU.

Between January and June of 2002, 15 per cent of all deliveries in Dublin were to non-nationals. In 2003, the three maternity hospitals—Holles Street, the Rotunda and the Coombe—estimated the number of non-national mothers at about 6,000. Chinese mothers living in Britain, some of them illegal, also went to hospitals in the North to have their babies. The child became an Irish citizen—even if both parents were illegal.

Among them was Levette Chen, who entered the UK in May 2000 when she was six months pregnant. Her daughter Catherine was born in a Belfast hospital in September 2000, earning the right to live anywhere in the EU. Not wishing to remain in Ireland, she took the baby to live with her husband and four-year-old son in Wales. She and her husband did not have the right of residency in either Ireland or Britain, but Catherine did.

The numbers forced the government to act. On June 11, 2004, it held a referendum on the 27th Amendment of the Constitution Act, which said: "A person born in the island of Ireland ... who does not have, at the time of birth, at least one parent who is an Irish citizen or entitled to be an Irish citizen, is not entitled to Irish citizenship or nationality, unless provided for by law." The public voted 79 per cent in favour; the amendment was signed into law on June 24. But it did not apply to those before the amendment was passed. There were 9,500 non-national parents whose children were born before the referendum. How many of these were Chinese we do not know but my guess is a substantial number. This "birth tourism" is big business in the United States; under its law, any child born there is an American citizen. For a substantial fee, a company takes expectant mothers from China to California, where they stay in company-run houses until and after the birth. Since Asian women are slimmer than Westerners, their pregnancy is often less visible to immigration officers at the airports.

One of the best known Chinese in Ireland is celebrity chef Chan Kwang-hi. He has lived in the country for forty years and represented the country at international events. In 2008, he won the silver medal at the Germany Culinary Olympics and, in 2014, the Laureat of Le Grand Prix de Cuisine de l'Academie Paris. Born in Hong Kong, Chan moved to Ireland in 1988 at the age of eight to live with his uncle in Buncrana, County Donegal, with its population of 4,500. His uncle ran a Chinese takeaway and restaurant, the only one in the town. "At the start, it was very hard to get people to try Chinese food for the first time. The Irish had a very basic diet—potatoes, meat and vegetables," he told me.

In 1996, he was accepted into a French catering college in a nearby town where he graduated three years later. Then he worked in some of the best restaurants in the country, under leading chefs. At the same time, he earned a B.Sc in International Culinary Arts by TVU London. For three and a half years, he was head chef in a Michelin-star restaurant which offered modern European cuisine with fresh seasonal Irish produce.

In 2015, he founded ChanChan Hong Kong Street Food Sauces in Dublin. It creates and produces spices and condiments that connect Irish food with Asian flavours. "I go back to Hong Kong every year and I love the street food. Every piece of street food comes with a sauce. You choose between five or six different ones." ChanChan sells its products to retail shops, supermarkets and restaurants in Dublin and other cities.

He wants to revolutionise the Chinese food of Ireland with more authentic flavours. Having spent most of his career preparing continental food, he wants to bring the best tastes and recipes of his native Hong Kong to his adopted country, because the Irish consumer is ready for this transformation.

There are more than 400 Chinese restaurants across the country, including about 100 in Dublin. While a small number are for connoisseurs, most serve take-aways and fast food. The majority of Irish people know little of the variety and sophistication of Chinese cuisine. That is what Chan plans to change. With a Chinese-American food writer, in 2016, he launched Slaint-Chi (想喫); slaint means 'good health' in Irish. "We want to bring the true flavours of Chinese food to Ireland," he told me.

Since 2012, Chinese have had a new channel to move to Ireland. This is the Investment Immigrant Programme (IIP), established by the Department of Justice and Equality (DJE) in 2012. It is similar to programmes offered by several countries – they do not require the applicant to move and have no language or academic bar nor age limit.

In February 2019, then Minister of Justice and Equality

Charles Flanagan told *The Dail* that, since 2012, the programme had raised more than 500 million euros of investment for the Irish economy, with Chinese accounting for 93 per cent of the approved applications.

"Applicants must be high net worth individuals with a personal wealth of at least €2 million and no criminal record," the rules state. The various options for visa-seeking investors including Enterprise Investment with a minimum of €1 million invested in an Irish enterprise, investment in approved real estate of more than €2 million, or a minimum €500,000 philanthropic donation to a project of public benefit to the arts, sports, health, culture or education in Ireland. Once an application is approved, the person is given permission to live in Ireland with his or her spouse and children under eighteen.

Hong Kong remains one of the wealthiest cities in the world and its population is very mobile. Many Chinese people, from Hong Kong and the mainland, want the security of a second passport; they fear political instability, state control of their currency and assets and, in the worst case scenario, a war between China and Taiwan. They want an escape route and to park assets overseas. Ireland allows dual nationality, so a Chinese who becomes a citizen does not have to give up his Chinese passport. Consultants in Hong Kong sell the Golden Visa by saying that Ireland is now, thanks to Brexit, the only English-speaking country in the European Union.

The website of Bartra Capital, one of these consultants, lists the benefits of an Irish passport—visa-free access to 185 countries, the only EU passport that allows the holder to live and work in the UK, the highest GDP growth rate in the EU, a tax rate of 12.5 percent at least until 2025, an education system ranked seventh in the world, the Silicon Valley of Europe with more than 1,000 large high-technology companies, top in the world for food safety and air quality. Dublin, Cork and Galway are ranked among the top friendliest cities in the world.

The Chinese presence in Ireland is young, less than seventy years old. The pioneers were the skilled cooks who prepared food that Irish people then scarcely dared to eat. While the cooks are still hard at work, they have been joined by men with ties and striped suits – bankers and executives of aircraft leasing firms, IT and biotech companies, computer engineers and fintech wizards. There are also doctors, accountants, architects, pastors and other professionals. Hazel Chu and Anna Lo were the first to cast off the low profile that Chinese migrants usually keep in foreign countries and stepped into the public arena. There they have met abuse and insults as well as praise and recognition. These new migrants are well-educated, confident and hard working. They can make the same contribution to their new country as the many Irish people have made in Asia.

Epilogue

Despite the country's remarkable economic progress since joining the European Union in 1973, Irish people continue to move abroad. They live in nearly all the countries of the EU as well as the traditional sites of emigration – Britain, U.S., Canada, Australia and Argentina. During the 19th and 20th century, no European country lost more people than Ireland – 1.25 million during the Great Famine of 1845-49 and a surge in the 1950s when nearly 15 per cent of the population left. The population in 2022 of 7.1 million was still below the pre-Famine figure of 8.18 million in 1841. There are an estimated 70 million people of Irish ancestry around the world, about half of them in the United States and including President Joe Biden. The Department of Foreign Affairs has an "Irish Abroad Unit" dedicated to look after this diaspora. Since 2004, it has made grants of more than 200 million euros to 530 organisations in 36 countries to its citizens overseas through its Emigrant Support Programme.

This history means that Irish people are global. They grow up listening to stories of family and friends who have emigrated. Lyrical and melancholy songs describe this painful exile and sense of loss – a migrant crushing stones in a penal colony in Australia dreams of the cliffs and mountains of his native County Kerry in the southwest of Ireland. Many people have relatives overseas who can help them if they wish to follow. During the summer, relatives from abroad come to visit the family at home. Abroad is not far away. Being a small country also helps; it keeps Irish people humble and laughing at themselves and encourages them to learn foreign languages. It is easier for citizens of big countries – Russia, China, U.S. and, thanks to their empires, Britain and France – to be arrogant.

Like those we have described in this book, many Irish people today want to experience life, work and culture in another country. But the migrants now are different to those of the 19th century. Since the introduction of free secondary schooling in 1967, education has blossomed. By 2020, 51 per cent of working-age adults had completed higher education. So the migrants of today are more likely to be IT or fin-tech specialists, accountants, nurses, doctors, engineers or teachers rather than the pedlars, road and rail builders and factory workers of a century ago.

Thanks and Acknowledgements

I MUST THANK many people for this book. Years ago, I learnt that writing a book is a collective, not an individual, enterprise. What you will read is the joint effort of dozens of people.

First, I must thank members of my family. I never met Grandfather Frederick, and his wife Annie only once. But I learnt enough to understand that they were remarkable people, living for four decades in a remote, cold town in northeast China. They inspired me to write *Frederick, the Life of my Missionary Grandfather in Manchuria,* which was published in 2012 by Joint Publishing of Hong Kong, with editions in English and Chinese, traditional and simplified. Then I must thank my father, a psychiatrist in London and an army doctor who received the Military Cross for bravery during World War Two. I remember his charm, his humour and his stories – firing the starting gun on my Irish journey.

When I lived in Manchester between 1973 and 1975, I stayed with Joe and Ann McMurray, a Scottish couple of Irish ancestry; warm and hospitable, they taught me much about the island "across the water". After I moved to Belfast in 1975, I had many teachers; I describe them in the book – Roisin McAuley, Reverend Jack Weir, Reverend John Dunlop and Father Des Wilson. All helped to guide the blind man through the forest. Despite – or because of – the Troubles, Belfast was full of humour; I salute the many joke-makers for their role in keeping everyone's spirits up. In the Republic, my principal teachers were the Gibbons family—Dr Hugh Gibbons TD and his children, especially Luke, Hugh Jr and Bernadette. Rev Weir, Father Wilson and Dr Gibbons have passed away. I remain in touch with the others, as much as is possible during a pandemic; they graciously revised and corrected the text.

In Asia, I have mainly lived in Hong Kong, Beijing, Tokyo and Shanghai. In all these cities, the Irish diplomats were always warm and helpful. In Beijing, Ambassador Declan Kelleher played a key role in two of my books, which you can read about in the text. In Shanghai, Consul-General Geoffrey Keating arranged many excellent cultural events at the Blarney Stone, the leading Irish pub in the city. We also spent weekends exploring historic sites and arguing over history at a restaurant overlooking the Huangpu river; I thank him for his precious time. Peter Ryan opened the Irish consulate in 2014. He supported my writing by organising book presentations; his invitation attracted a much larger audience than mine would have. In 2018, he was replaced by David Costello. He graciously invited me to help him with a history of the Irish in Hong Kong, from its foundation in 1841. That was a project from heaven—a chance to research the lives of governors, soldiers, priests, lawyers, policemen and entrepreneurs and meet many of the community here. In June 2013, the Department of Foreign Affairs kindly invited me to give a presentation of Grandfather's book at its headquarters in Iveagh House, St Stephen's Green. It attracted a large audience of Irish diplomats and scholars and Chinese officials. The department made a generous donation toward the cost of writing the book and bought 180 copies. This endorsement greatly helped in promotion work.

It is due to all these teachers that I have been able to travel a long distance in search of my Irish history and identity. I thank them all very much.

About The Author

Mark O'Neill was born in London to a Northern Irish father and an English mother. He was educated at Marlborough College and New College, Oxford and became a journalist, working in Washington DC, Manchester and Belfast, before moving to Hong Kong in 1978. He has lived in Asia ever since, working in Taiwan, India, China, Japan and Hong Kong. Since 2006, he has concentrated on writing books, of which "*Out of Ireland*" is the 14th.

Milton Keynes UK
Ingram Content Group UK Ltd.
UKHW041504240823
427430UK00004B/75